Smudge's Story

The story of an East End lad
who served in the Royal Navy in the First World War

Copyright © 2014
Wendy Reader and Graham Rogers
All rights reserved.
ISBN-13: 978-1495253430
ISBN-10: 1495253430

Foreword by Wendy Reader – joint editor

Fred Smith, or "Smudge" as he was known, was a lovely grandfather. I remember him playing the piano by ear –a mystery to me when I was a young child and struggling with sight-reading and piano exams. He could also sketch and shade pencil drawings of people, pets and scenes. He could connect telephone extensions, so that we could talk to each other around the house – and he grew hundreds of geranium cuttings – the scent of which I loathed.

He surprised me by turning up at Cork harbour in August 1967 – when he was 73 – to join the ship on which I was travelling home after a year at High School in Massachusetts. He told me that he had been, "paying his respects to Cork". I regret now that I did not ask the true reason for his journey to Ireland. In hindsight, I can now see that this was when he was busy writing his account of his First World War naval service and obviously wanted to return to Ireland. The photo below is of me, Fred and my mother – his only child Rosina Alice Louisa – when we arrived in Southampton docks the next day.

This account of his early years and service in the Royal Navy during and after the First World War was found in his home after his death in 1970. It was written during the late 1960s in exercise books, after his beloved wife Louisa had died. He used some old diaries, which are no longer around, and his own memory. As far as we know, he did not share his thoughts, and, of course, it is now impossible to ask him more details about what he saw and did.

Along with many postcards, drawings and photos, my mother, my cousin Graham Rogers and I donated a copy of his account to the Imperial War Museum shortly before she died in 2002.

The cost of the First World War in human lives was horrific. More than 65 million men and women fought, of whom more than half were killed or injured. In the UK, there was barely a family that did not lose at least one family member.

As we remember the 1914–1918 War today – a hundred years have passed – but we should never forget those who fought on land or sea – or on the home-front. This story is dedicated to them and to the memory of Fred Smith – "Smudge".

Wendy, Fred and Rosina
in Southampton 1967

Foreword by Graham Rogers – joint editor

When I was eight, my father took me to see his Uncle Fred, then in his late sixties. My enduring memory is of him in his greenhouse full of cacti. About ten years ago his granddaughter Wendy showed me his autobiography and it has fascinated me ever since.

Fred was a working class boy from a poor background who left school at the age of fourteen. He succeeded in the Navy and many years later wrote an account of his early years and his time in the Navy, from 1913 to 1920. In my experience, such war memoirs from the lower ranks are few and far between.

I was born just after the Second World War, not far from Fred's birthplace and have been fortunate enough to have lived through a time of relative peace. Perhaps this makes me even more willing to echo Fred's amazement when he writes, "It is now, in my old age, I wonder how I endured, and how anyone might endure such things."

Things like his grinding poverty in the East End and the day, when still a child he collected five-thousand cherry stones and, with the money he got for them, bought his mother a brooch only to find her, the night before her birthday, alone at home and dying. Then, after joining the Navy, there was the night when he was nearly swept off his tiny ship by huge Atlantic waves and alone on the deck he clung to freezing ropes. He was haunted by memories of the scared faces he had seen in mountainous seas, the screams of terrified people trapped behind portholes of sinking ships and by the desperate cries of the thousands of refugees trying to flee the Russian Revolution by boarding his ship, icebound in the Odessa harbour. But then there were the reunions with his family and Louisa, the love of his life.

Perhaps you too might pause, as Fred did – for what a panorama of events he unfolds...

Graham Rogers 2014

Notes

This book has been published through CreateSpace Self Publishing by Wendy Reader and Graham Rogers, with the help of other members of Fred's extended family.

News about this book and can be found at:

www.SmudgesStory.co.uk

The editors may be contacted at:

SmudgesStory@gmail.com

Acknowledgements

We are grateful to the following for help with this book: Wendy's mother Rosina Robinson née Smith, for not throwing the papers away! To Wendy's husband, Den Reader[*] for his fantastic support and for producing such excellent covers for the book. Wendy's sister-in-law, Diane Reader Sorrells for her support and for helping with the initial transcribing and typing of the story. To "Let's Talk" magazine[†] for their support in publishing excerpts in 2013 and 2014, which provided an impetus to publish the whole story. To various members of the Smith and Haswell families for verifying facts, dates and identifying some of the people in the pictures. To Graham's cousins, Wendy Woods and Yvonne Feekery for helping identify some of the babies in the pictures. To Tim and Valerie Rogers for their advice and help. To the Imperial War Museum for checking certain facts (a copy of Fred's original document together with many pictures was donated to them in 2002). And finally, to Fred Smith – Smudge, himself – for leaving such an interesting and well-written account of his early life and service.

Wendy Reader, Norfolk
Graham Rogers, Fordingbridge
2014
www.smudgesstory.co.uk

---

[*] www.denreader.com
[†] www.letstalk24.com

Contents

Foreword by Wendy Reader – joint editor iii

Foreword by Graham Rogers – joint editor v

Notes vi

Acknowledgements vii

Chapter 1 – Preface 1

Chapter 2 – The Early Years 1894-1901 3

Chapter 3 – 1901–1908 School, a stepfather and strikes. 9

Chapter 4 – 1908 The Tragedy of my Life 21

Chapter 5 – Street life 25

Chapter 6 – Working life and learning a trade 31

Chapter 7 – 1913 Joining the Navy 37

Chapter 8 – First Posting HMS Derwent 51

Chapter 9 – War, HMS Kale and an injury 59

Chapter 10 – HMS Jessamine 71

Chapter 11 – Rescue of the SS Ausonia 77

Chapter 12 – Minesweeping 89

Chapter 13 – Home leave... and romance blossoms 93

Chapter 14 – Engagement rings and trouble in Ireland 105

Chapter 15 – Rescue of SS California and a wedding! 113

Chapter 16 – Promotion and HMS Ceres 123

Chapter 17 – The Armistice and SS Cassandra 135

Chapter 18 – To Riga and the rescue of Mrs Hill 151

Chapter 19 – HMS Ceres to the Mediterranean 159

Chapter 20 – Yugoslavia 165

Chapter 21 – Summer in Malta 183

Chapter 22 – Gibraltar 189

Chapter 23 – Autumn in Turkey 195

Chapter 24 – Africa 205

Chapter 25 – Russia and news from home. 213

Postscript 229

Appendix i Family Tree 233

Appendix ii Fred's Naval Record 234

Appendix iii Alfred Bence 235

Dedicated to the memory
of my grand-father
Frederick Smith
"Smudge"
1894 – 1970

Wendy Reader 2014

Chapter 1 – Preface

As I pause to write this story, what a panorama of events comes to mind from half a century ago. Some say life is full of ups and downs. My apologies if my story appears crude, I am not an author just someone who has experienced the grave and gay side of life. I did not keep a proper diary, and so I have not mentioned the dates of many of these events. I am just relating incidents of interest, as my memory will permit. You see these happenings were fifty years ago now, so I am recalling what I can and in as simple a pattern as possible. They are memories that will remain forever indelibly in my mind.

Little did I think that I would ever be a husband, let-alone a grandfather. After all, one can only live in the present and not the future but the past is an undisputed fact.

As one gets older, and perhaps wiser, one is apt to see so many people, perhaps too many, grasping at the shadow and forgetting the substance, the real essence of life.

It is sometimes hard to take knocks but successes compensate to give one a lovely feeling of self-confidence. To be confident in myself has been my main endeavour. That, and always to be willing to be guided by those who love us. But what if nobody is there to guide, comfort or show us love? Then we must fight a lone battle with destiny, always looking for reassurance and wondering if in the great unknown, or unseen, there is a guide.

Sidcup 1967

Chapter 2 – The Early Years 1894-1901

My father George William Smith married Ella Hawkins in 1882[c]. He died in 1898 when I was about four years of age, and all I knew about him was that at one time he was a prosperous greengrocer in East London. However, I am afraid his downfall was drink and, more so, his associates. That is the reason I am always mindful and wary of that pattern of friendship. I was the youngest of the four children my dear mother was left with. I was born in August 1894, in West Ham. My brother George, four years older than me, was my inseparable comrade throughout my life until he died in the 1950s. My sisters Ella and Beatrice were nine and eleven years older than I was.

My earliest recollection was of the squalid surroundings at 38 Warmington Street, Plaistow where we lived. There we had just two rooms, one of which was very small. We also had the use of a scullery. For all of that we paid about one shilling and sixpence a week in rent. Our living room was also the bedroom for my mother and sisters. How can I describe this sordid home? Or perhaps I should say, humble home. We had a paraffin oil lamp; there was no electricity in those days and hardly any gas. The oil lamp had to be cleaned every day; otherwise, the light would have been awfully dull. We took pride in a clean glass chimney on the lamp and we always had to be on guard not to jolt the table or knock the lamp over. We had a coal-fired range on which we did the cooking.

It was a common sight, in those days, to see families doing what we called a moonlight flit. Although the rents were low, many were unable to pay them and so ran into debt. Hence, late at night mums, dads and kids could be seen pushing coster's barrows with their precious belongings on top. The gas streetlamps had no mantles, because they used Bray burners. These were very dim and so the people would move by moonlight, whilst hoping their neighbours would not see them.

---

[c] There is a family tree in Appendix i

There were always rooms to let in every street and in this way people hoped to eke out their meagre incomes. However, it is sad to say, the pubs were always flourishing. What a strange world it is.

My real recollections start when I was about seven. I remember my dear mother. She worked long hours, about ten hours a day, at Badgers in Stepney emptying barrels of ginger for about ten shillings a week. A man's wage at that time was about eighteen shillings a week. She walked a long way to work. Public transport was by horse-tram or horse-bus, the fares of which were ha'penny a mile. Workmen's fares were tuppence return for four miles. "That's cheap," you might say. Mother would arrive home after 7.30 p.m. and although tired would then see about our food. Food was really our greatest problem.

We would sometimes go to the market and see what we could get when nobody was looking. While two or three created a nuisance the others, if they were lucky, would sneak away some fruit. At our age, and because of our need, we did not consider this to be a sin. I thought it was the answer to my prayers, because my mother made me say, "Give us this day our daily bread." Was He guiding us? Anyway, I am not ashamed of my lapses, which were all through necessity. My mother believed in bringing us up in a Christian way, but how difficult that was.

A two-pound loaf of bread was three-ha'pence. It was weighed out, which meant we often got a piece of bread for a makeweight. I was always willing to run errands for anybody. On the way home, if there was bread, I would usually eat the makeweight and then say it was the correct weight. "A lie", you say, but what would you do if you were hungry? And in those days I was often hungry.

A pound of margarine was tuppence-ha'penny, while butter was so expensive it was out of the question. Five pound of potatoes cost tuppence. A pound of pot-herbs, our name for carrots, onions, turnips and the like, was a ha'penny, and that would be enough for us.

Tea was ten pence a pound for the cheapest but my share would be a second watering from the tealeaves. A pound of sugar was three-ha'pence and milk a penny a pint. We had condensed milk from a tin as it lasted longer and was cheap at three-ha'pence a tin.

The milkman had a 16-gallon churn on a handcart to deliver milk to housewives. In the early days they had to bring out jugs or basins, but later on they had special milk cans, which housewives had to keep clean themselves from day to day. There were no milk bottles at that time. Nothing was pre-packed; butter, tea and sugar were weighed out by the shopkeeper for each customer.

Our daily meals would be as follows: for breakfast we just had bread and marge, or sometimes oatmeal porridge, but without milk. For our main meal, usually in the evening, and if we had some money, we would get tuppence worth of pieces and ask for a piece of kidney; such was our cheek. One could get a pennyworth of marrowbones, half a pennyworth of trotters, three-ha'pence of scrag of mutton and chops for tuppence each. This was all very succulent and delicious meat with plenty of nourishment, but at a price. A good solid meal could be had for a few coppers, but where were those valuable coppers to be found?

Our life, however, seemed to get more difficult, and so my mother managed to get a mangle on hire purchase for sixpence a week. We kept this in the landlady's scullery and George and I went into business. We canvassed the neighbours and did their mangling for a penny a dozen items. I put them in because I was young and small, while George turned the handle. We were delighted to add a few coppers to the kitty. But still Mother had money troubles and we could not keep up the payments on the mangle. The shopkeeper, who was also a Justice of the Peace, heard my mother's story and forgave the debt.

How my mother managed, I shall never know. She always looked tired and worried. Then my sister Ella got a job as a waitress at a restaurant named "Cere" in the Minories. "Hurrah," we all said. (You will read later how the name *Ceres* played a big part in my naval career). Now, knowing our needs, and problems,

Ella soon managed to fetch home food, which had been left uneaten by the customers. Ella would have her share at the shop, and I would meet her at Plaistow station and rummage through her bag to see what she had. Sometimes it was blancmange or custard pies and I would think that I was in fairyland and eat some on the way home, but I would always have to remember the others. In this way our desperate food situation was eased. I was getting on nicely at school, and when I was aged about eight I begin to take stock of my clothing. My clothes were all hand-me-downs, all well patched and airy with holes. We were certainly rough necks. My footwear was deplorable as well, because second-hand boots cost one shilling to one-and-six a pair. So it was save, save; and save in farthings. This meant going without sweets. Sweets, by the way, were as cheap as three-ha'pence a pound, and a farthing's worth could be shared between us boys. We learned never to be selfish. Toffee apples were four a penny. But we had to look forward to some luck coming our way if we wanted money for sweets.

    Boys and girls, and lots of them, would play in the freezing wet streets in their bare feet, and would become blue with the cold. In the coldest weather we would have races and all sorts of jumping games. There were no fires at home until the evening because of the cost of coal, which was eleven pence for a hundredweight or eighteen shillings a ton. Matches, however, were only about a penny for a dozen boxes. Us children would find some old rags or socks, from a dustbin, then get a jam tin, punch holes in the bottom with a nail, tie some string to it and ram the rags in the tin. We would then set light to it and swing it around on the string to make it burn, and then take turns to hold it to warm our hands. With the smell and the smoke it was shocking.

    Sometimes we would stand in pub doorways and get a little warmth, until our parents came home at night time. It was a common sight on Friday nights, which were pay-nights, for wives to call their husbands from the pubs in order get their housekeeping money before it all went on booze. There were, of course, arguments and fights galore. Shall I just call it our variety night because there was never a dull moment? If mothers were ill they would send their children to stand outside the pub, or even open the door and appeal to their fathers to, "Please come home." But usually this was to no avail. At that early age, I got a very deep impression of how cruel parents could be. Yet, I suppose, for those not being able to cope at home, it was a coward's way out.

Now perhaps you can well understand why I have so much sympathy for the weaker sex. Sympathy for women who are not credited enough for their untiring efforts on behalf of their children, whilst keeping loyalty to bestial husbands. Of course, in human nature, there will always be the black sheep. Maybe in desperation some choose outlets in drink, or just lose their balance of control. I find today that it is easy to criticise, yet harder to do any better. It was only too true that in my young days many people had no room for Christianity. How could they believe the platitudes preached from the pulpit? We learned at Sunday school that, "All good things around us are sent from Heaven above." However, we had hardly seen a tree or garden. We had seen plenty of ragged clothes, hungry bellies, fathers quarrelling with mothers and lots of squalor. We did not even have any fires to keep us warm. So, we would say, "What are these things from Heaven above?"

It all looks like a tragic picture that I am conveying, but that was a Cockney's way of life. Our clothing was always shabby and usually bought at the second-hand stall in the market place or a jumble sale or even came from dustbins. We were literally scroungers. But oh, the excitement, if one of us made a real capture. Sometimes a Sunday school teacher would favour me with articles of apparel that could be altered by poor old Mother, who had more than her share of hardship. I will always revere her memory. She was the epitome of loveliness to me and someone I always obeyed implicitly. As I have said, how she managed I will never know. Was it a mother's instinct? It was more than duty. How I have missed her guidance.

Now, to leave nostalgic emotion for a moment. Let me tell you about my life in those days.

Chapter 3 – 1901–1908 School, a stepfather and strikes.

My mother re-married a German named Claus Schroder. He was a kindly sort of man and was handy at any job. Jobs like making keys, repairing locks or mending kids hoops, with a forge he had made in the back yard. With the aid of a curved piece of iron, called a skimmer, we could roll our hoops all round the streets. We kept a few chickens in the back yard, and sold the eggs to neighbours. Stepfather was a stoker at the Gas Works at Beckton and when he was on night shift I used to take his supper to him. I think he liked me and he used to show me how gas was made. We had gas lighting and one gas ring in the house at that time. It is to my stepfather I owe a debt of gratitude, in that he showed me how to do jobs of all sorts, and that knowledge has stood me in good stead all my life. I watched him repair shoes and even mend old and disreputable prams. I learnt fast. I also took to drawing and became quite good; at least, so people used to say.

My stepfather already had two daughters and we all moved to Canning Town to a small house in Clarkson Street. Mum packed up her job and I had to change schools. At my new school, an even dingier one, I started doing very well indeed. I began going to Malvern College Mission, a tiny tin church, where I joined a boys club. There I learned gymnastics and drilling. It was great fun for me. I also joined the choir, my voice not being too shocking, but the best thing was that I was now earning my first wages. In a full quarter, I would get seven shillings and sixpence. My word, I was somebody and of course, by now, I was a real churchgoer, every evening and three times on Sunday. But what it was all about I had no idea. The sermons were boring, as was the constant muttering of prayers, which to me, as a lad, were too monotonous. I suppose I thought I was becoming holy, or something, in my cassock and surplice. Mum would always say, "Now wash your neck and behind your ears." So, I had to look the part and the picture of innocence. Our vicar had been a missionary and I thought he was marvellous, and I really grew to love him. He visited my mother and she was pleased that I was in good hands. We then had a new parson, who was, as my mother said, High Church of England, and he added all sorts of queer things to the services, much to the dislike of many. The choirboys were taught new hymns and carols, which were to be sung in Latin. Goodness knows what we were singing. My mother asked me once, in the presence of neighbours, to sing a carol or two, so I burst forth in Latin. I will not quote what she said, but it was a real Cockney flourish meaning 'enough of that', then she said, "The idea, of it, giving kids that stuff to learn!" The parson was promptly told his fortune and left the Mission. In some ways I was sorry, "Why was the parson so silly," I thought, "to upset good honest and poor people?" As young as I was, I can tell you, it got me thinking. I changed churches and joined the Congregational church. But they had no choir there. My income was slashed and my attendance was not so frequent, but it was more down to earth. When I prayed it was my own thoughts and not read from a book. I could be more up to date and pray from my own heart. I did not need university parsons expounding their ideas. How could they know what real hardship and poverty meant to us? I doubted they could. You may think that I am preaching, but I am not really.

My church life did one thing for me, which lasted throughout my life. It gave me a moral understanding of fellow beings with all their goodness and faults and during my life I have held that balance. I have always tried to be tolerant and to remember that, "to err is human; to forgive is divine".

By now, my mother was jogging along and life was a little easier, but my stepsisters were real tomboys and the bane of her life. They were a little older than me, real tough wenches and as strong as lions. I was scared to upset them and I am afraid they caused endless rows. It rather put my clock back and I became an outdoor urchin playing football in the streets with balls made of rags and string, and cricket with a piece of wood for a bat and a lamppost for a wicket. My stepsisters would play our games, even jumping over backs, and woe betide any boy who cheated or upset them. One of them particularly would fight like a savage, whilst I was a bit demure. The other kids were afraid of her, and so was my mother. This particular sister liked to be hypnotised by the boys who were always teasing her. I used to stand by and say to myself, "Watch it Freddie boy, panic stations will soon begin". My word she used to flail those kids. I would keep at a distance but all she would say was, "I was under the 'fluence." After that she would become normal again and a battle royal would take place when stockings and undies would be torn, which was never a very elegant sight. She would then go home to cause more turmoil and rows.

About this time, when I was about eight years of age, my sister Ella got married to a house decorator named Ernest Rogers. They lived nearby but it was a blow to us, because we were left to manage, without our treats.

I can remember one Christmas when I had been practising carols at the church. It must have reminded my mother because on Christmas morning I found a stocking – or an apology for one – hanging on my bed with an orange, an apple, a little bag of sweets and a small card in it. It was Mum's effort and greatly appreciated by me. I thought such things could not happen to me.

My sister Ella then had her first baby, who they named Ernest. My mum would send me around to her house at weekends to mind the baby, do the shopping and other minor jobs for Ella. I thought they were rich because they had a mail cart, which was a contraption for taking the baby out for walks, and could be used for carrying shopping. I became a part-time drudge, scrubbing stairs and steps, cleaning knives (not as easy as the stainless steel ones of today), black-leading the large stove, shopping and taking the baby out. All for a penny. Whacked out, on the way home, I would get a ha'penny, worth of chips from a fish and chip shop. That is probably why chips still attract me to this day.

At that time I do not remember hearing one word of endearment and never had a loving hug or kiss. Everything was so matter of fact. Perhaps people were too worried and harassed, by trying to make ends meet, to spare a little sentiment. I used to think to myself, "How can one be sure of being loved without some demonstration?" It means such a great deal and is so heart-warming in any human being's life and it costs nothing. If only I could have been reassured, but alas it was not to be. I was a little perplexed, especially as some of our neighbours would sometimes give me a hug or a kiss. Was it any wonder I was puzzled? But I have now accepted the fact that it was our hardships and stresses that made my family unable to give vent to their emotions. Maybe I was thought silly in expecting so much. Was I? I wonder.

I keep going into lapses of emotion, while I am trying to be factual and explicit, but it is all part of my story.

My sister Beatrice married a comedian named Philip Simister. He was also a dock labourer in the Royal Albert Docks. He used to make us laugh with his funny songs, and what a thing a sense of humour was in those days. They lived in one upstairs room. What a motley throng our family were.

Beatrice went a bit wild, she had a nasty temper and our environment did not help. But she could also be very loving. When blaming anybody for straying off the straight and narrow path I sometimes have to think of what I would have done. It was another of those perplexities that made me think very deeply, even at that young age.

Now about school, which I really loved. I was eager to learn and made rapid progress. My teachers were excellent, although I did get whackings with the big cane. Sometimes this was for loyalty to my mates, but I was never bad enough to be caned on my backside, or at least, so the teachers thought. They were moulding me the right way to face the world, for which I shall always be grateful. I can still say, with feeling, "Thank you, Sirs." The school was a dingy building where the three Rs – reading, writing and arithmetic – were drummed into us and which I lapped up and retained. Because of that, I was soon top of the form, as they say. My teachers were very interested in me and so I gave of my best, which pleased my mother very much.

I loved sums and geometry but the best lesson was on Friday afternoons and called general information. We could write a question on a slate hanging in the classroom and if the teacher could not answer it he gave us sixpence. The teachers would also write a question on the slate each week and if we got the answer right they would give us threepence. Well, this became very amusing and the funny answers would evoke lots of laughter, a wonderful boost before our dull weekends. I was always an inquisitive boy and I thought up a question, which lots of kids might ask and never get the same answer. Clever me wrote, "Where do doctors get their babies from?" I had frequently seen the doctor going into a house with a black bag and often noticed a new baby appeared, soon after. It made me think. This question caused giggles and curiosity among staff and children. Friday afternoon came and I wondered if I would get the tanner. The teacher took down the slate and said, "Fred Smith has won the prize; I could have answered, but I shall not do so." Cor! Was I excited! I bought half a pound of sweets for three-ha'pence, scrambled them amongst the kids and saved the rest of the money.

I will now insert the sequel to this tale, which is relevant. After I joined the Royal Navy, I visited my old school one day, in my smart uniform with a blue jacket. My old teacher was still there and he took me into the staff room along with the headmaster and said,

"Now Smith, I am going to answer your question of some years ago."

"Don't bother Sir," I said, "I know the answer now." and I offered him his sixpence back, which he refused to accept.

Sometimes, the three top boys were invited back to our teacher's home to have a high-tea, which was hot cakes, jam, blancmange and the like. To us kids, this was smashing.

All side streets of our area were just dirt, or rather earth mixed with granite chips, and pavements were of stone or bricks. The main roads were better, with granite blocks. All vehicles had tyres made of iron bands and were horse-drawn, or pulled by donkeys. It was quite common to see goods moved manually. It must be obvious that in dry weather the roads were very dusty, making everything grimy and dull and when it rained they turned into quagmires of mud and puddles.

I was about seven years old when the Boer War ended, but I can recall that us children, especially boys, would dress up with newspaper hats and swords made out of bits of wood from the shops, anything that cost nothing, and we would march about singing the war songs of the day. Perhaps we would challenge the next street and have our own war, which usually ended with casualties and tears. Then, as an aftermath, the parents would start scrapping, championing their own dear boys, who were so cherubic when on their best behaviour, yet so sadistic when in groups. Just like boys in the present day, I suppose. But is that instinct or do boys just think it is what boys do? Little girls were not always angels and they could be terrors as well.

What else could we do? We were inventive with games and we excelled at scrounging or borrowing. Can you imagine an environment devoid of radio, television and cinemas? In fact, for us, there was no entertainment at all. So, it was a case of idle hands find mischief.

My most marvellous sight was the magic lantern, which was very crude at first, but it amused us kids. We gambled with buttons, played with marbles on the pavements, collected cherry stones and devised games with them to meet our gambling instinct. There were plenty of games to play, such as Knocking Down Ginger. We would run down the road and knock on someone's door, which was easy because there were no front gardens. Some householders might lie in wait and then woe betides the slowest runner. He would get a beating with a belt on his backside. Fortunately I was a good runner.

I was no angel, except to my mum, bless her. She would always forgive my misdeeds, provided I spoke the truth. There is a moral there, I think, and I hope.

Now to another change in my life. I began to feel I was wanted by the way my brother George always moved around with me, although he had older boys for pals, he watched over me. Even the publican's son, just across the road from us, asked me to his home to play with him. I thought it seemed that he had a toyshop all to himself. He had clockwork trains, toys and games of all sorts. Best of all was the good grub I was given when visiting there, and the gifts of leftover clothing. I was feeling so posh that I started to buy white paper collars, at a farthing each. So now I must, perforce, wash my neck more often! It is laughable when I think of it now. I must thank that mum from the pub for brightening my drab life. God bless her, even if she was a publican, she was a Christian.

About this time there was trouble at the Docks and thousands of men would muster near my home holding rowdy meetings. The big ships that came into the London Docks supplied all the London markets. Us kids would go and listen at the meetings but had not the foggiest idea what it was all about. It was the beginning of the Trade Unions in Dockland. The speakers were working men who were rebelling against their conditions. Their charter was called The Dockers Tanner, meaning that they were asking for sixpence an hour. Hours worked per week were of a casual nature, perhaps only two or three days a week and there was neither unemployment pay nor sickness benefit. There were relieving officers who would apply a means test but before you could receive anything you were expected to pawn your furniture, household linen and clothing, to buy food. It worked like this: Monday morning there would be queues at the pawnshop of women with bed linen, cheap jewellery, many with wedding rings, mother's coat, frocks and father's best suit. All would be offered up as collateral for a loan of money. On this interest had to be paid weekly and these rates were high. Goods were valued by the pawnbroker, which were perhaps a quarter of their real value, and a pawn ticket would be issued. If people's misfortune lingered on and the interest mounted, some articles would never be redeemed. But habits were such that, if father had not been dragged out of a pub quick enough on Friday night, it was in Monday and out Friday.

During this time it really was a sad state of affairs with pilfering, scrounging and stealing all rampant. There were gaunt stern faces wherever you went, and queues for the soup kitchens. The Salvation Army was at its best and I raise my hat to them. Most men and women lost their dignity and the worry of their children made them drawn and haggard. Thank God I was not driven to extremes.

Can you imagine what my prayers were as a young lad? I was never more in earnest and always hoped against hope for an answer. If I had an answer it must have been years after. Some poor devils had to be put in workhouses because the landlords had ejected them. There, they had at least shelter from the elements but the food was horrible and they were expected to do chores. How forlorn hope must have been. Not having any experience in workhouses I cannot say more, only that they were the most demoralising places, knocking out any vestige of hope the poor souls could ever have possessed.

In those days, even with all the misery and hardship, we had our do-gooders, as there are today. They were those humble and meek people who, seeking no publicity, were happy to end their days unsung and without honours, glory or titles. Content that their only reward was a warm satisfaction in their hearts. Even if some did accrue riches, they would be sure to use their wealth to give a helping hand. Yes, there were the Good Samaritans who did their utmost against a background of despair, which sometimes provoked desperate measures. There arose men like John Burns, Ben Tillett and Will Thorne to mention a few and there were many others. These men were dedicated to the workers in the Docks and they would lecture at street corners, or where space permitted, urging the men to tighten their belts and be prepared to starve and refuse to unload the food at the Docks.

Following the Dockers' strike, came the Great Strike. Tempers became frayed and the men became desperate and determined. Food vans were attacked and looted, and men became savage. My stepfather was able to keep working and I was a silent onlooker. The police were looked upon with disfavour. They were everywhere but could not cope with the looting and fighting. Men were afraid to blackleg and this caused untold bitterness and hatred even in the families. Us kids just couldn't understand it all. Trades people were in a sorry state as well, having to protect their shops and letting people have food on tick until better days arrived. Things really got bad and the Government was worried, so an emergency was proclaimed and the army brought in. Food vans were formed into convoys and drivers had an armed soldier with them. Mounted police were armed with batons, which they used freely, when keeping watch at meetings. Troops were not allowed to fire until the Riot Act was read, but starving men would be no match for the soldiers. But some of those soldiers may have been sons of the strikers. How would the troops react? They had two duties, one allegiance to the Crown, and the other loyalty to their kith and kin. Happily, this contingency did not arise and the strikers were calmed down by the mention of the Riot Act. Casualties were numerous and curses as well. I well remember one leader asking a huge crowd to bare their heads and listen. He uttered a prayer for the men and their families and ended with, "May God strike Lord Davenport dead." He was the chairman of the Port of London Authority and spokesman for the employers. Even the children would chant this in the streets.

For us kids, the limits of our travels were local and it was hard to visualise the green countryside or the open sea. I would hear stories from the others but I am afraid that did not comfort me and I thought, 'there must be hope somewhere.' Even the songs of those days always seemed to be sad ballads. These were lovely but they were tear-jerkers and made people cry.

My memory is vague about the length of the strike but if only a day it was too long. It must have lasted for a number of weeks. The fortitude, doggedness and patience that was shown, despite hungry bellies, brought forth the best in people. It had to be seen to be believed. More fortunate neighbours would get cheap nourishing stews and bread, as much as they could afford, and then gave it to others, sometimes going without themselves. Can a human being do more? That example, strange enough, is still followed. It takes the stresses and dangers of life to bring out the best in humans, if only it lasted throughout life, this comradeship, unselfishness and desire to help others but this must be a utopian dream.

I remember one of my mates in Sunday school asking our teacher, after he had read something from the Bible, "Please sir, do the rich people go to church and listen to Bible readings like we do?" And the teacher said,

"Of course they do."

"Well," my mate replied, "they don't take any notice of what Jesus says, do they? It seems funny to me. I'm sorry, but I don't understand." Words coming from youngsters sometimes have a ring of truth. The hierarchy of the church with all their affluence and pomp and splendour living in comfort, please take note. The original Leader would not have tolerated their conduct which is unbecoming of the times. One proverb, which I remember is, "Precepts may lead, but examples must follow." How apt, but who am I? Just a voice in the wilderness crying out for guidance on many things. I am unshaken and not ashamed and all through life I will endeavour to spread a little happiness, which pays dividends, and I have a contented mind.

Well, I must get down from my pulpit now and leave you to your own reasoning. Another sermon over. Now to revert to the story again.

The strike ended, the men won their case and the Docks resumed their normal activity. Slowly people began redeeming their goods from the pawnbrokers who were booming.

I was top of my class at school. My sister Beat moved home and had a baby but we did not see much of them. She was a silly girl. She could have been a pupil teacher but she was a romantic and wanted some happier life. "Well," I ask you, "wouldn't you want the same if you came from that background?" However, she drifted into a hum-drum life of a docker's wife. Her husband was a fine chap though, with a good physique. He had to be strong carrying quarters of beef of two or three hundredweight each. He was a non-smoker, just a moderate drinker and not a drunkard.

Ella now had two children; Horace had been born in 1905, which meant extra chores for me but no extra wages. At church I got on very well and begun to get to know my mates' parents – some poor and some not so poor. We were a mixed bunch of lads. I became the leader of a gymnastics team that had a vaulting horse, which became my favourite. There were also horizontal and parallel bars, clubs and we did Swedish drill and acrobatics. We were preparing for a display at the Town Hall and I was to be the leader. Imagine that, little insignificant me, at such a big event. I felt like a bighead. Three days before the display, or thereabouts, the physical instructor fell ill and the organisers were perturbed about this. Brother George suggested I take the boys on stage myself, and act as leader to prompt the boys by signs and words of command. After a rehearsal at this it was decided that the show must go on. I was given a singlet and cream flannel trousers and rubber shoes. The outfit really boosted my ego, and now I was really the part.

Chapter 4 – 1908 The Tragedy of my Life

On the last day of May 1908 it would be my mother's birthday. With the money I had got from 5,000 cherry stones I had picked up I bought her a brooch for a present. I think the stones were used to make dolls' eyes. A few days before Mum's birthday, we had done the final rehearsal and I was looking forward to the gymnastic display night. I was at home when I heard a bump from upstairs. I went up and found Mum had collapsed. On my own I laid her down to be as comfortable as possible, while I was wondering what to do next because I could not lift her you see. Strange to say, I did not panic. She revived a little and I remembered from my first-aid lessons to keep her warm. She opened her eyes and feebly asked for a cup of tea. I rushed downstairs and asked a neighbour to make a cup of tea whilst I went back to comfort Mum. I thought she must have had a fit but she looked so cold and then she had another fit, which proved to be apoplexy. Another neighbour rushed for a doctor and several people came in. I was cuddling Mum hoping that my brother George would come home from work; he was now an office boy. Well, Mum rallied again and asked for George. When the Doctor arrived I asked to stay and so it was that I was with her when she passed away. I hoped she had gone to get her reward for all she had done for us. When George arrived home he was stunned. We were both affected by deep emotion, shedding many tears.

As I write this, nearly sixty years later, my eyes are not dry thinking of that day when I lost all that was dear to me. My image had gone. Where now could I go for comfort and solace?

My stepfather arrived home, held us two boys, and tried to comfort us. I remember saying that I could not go to the Town Hall for the gymnastic display. He waited for my tears to subside and later, when I was more composed, he told me to be a brave little boy and gave me a pep talk that did me the power of good. "Look Son," he said, "this display tomorrow, what do you say about it?"

"I can't go Dad, can I?" I said.

"Who said so? Look, Son, you go and do your best. Don't let your mates and the audience down, and when you have done that come home and tell your mother about it. I'm sure that's what she would have wished for. Besides, it might help to ease your sorrow. Good luck to you."

Well, the day of the display arrived. What should I do? Reluctantly, I decided to go. My mates, via the jungle telegraph, had heard my sad news and understood my present mood. I did not want anybody to commiserate with me because I was really keyed up, but I would do my best.

The show started with three of four hundred people. Luckily, they were oblivious to me; otherwise, I should have been too shy. Anyway, the senior girls started with callisthenics. They were wearing gymslips and long stockings, because bare legs were indecent in those days. They received a great round of applause. Now I was really on edge. Would I flop? The piano tinkled out our music, and I was ready. I led the boys, they knew everything by heart, so for me, it was just a matter of timing all the exercises. I gradually grew more confident and even without a proper instructor we managed very well and were all applauded very generously. Boys and girls alternated with their turns. How I managed to get through with the apparatus exercises, I do not know. But I was playing a part and a voice in my head would keep saying, "Don't let the boys down, Smudge."

We survived the ordeal, and with some credit. We received the usual praise from the platform by a local councillor, and after the show I went home. Despite despair coming over me again, I had done as my stepfather had suggested. I went into the room where Mum was lying and in the candlelight I bowed my head. "I done it Mum," I said. For a while, I stood in silence and in tears. Then I said some prayers and kissed her, my last goodnight kiss. Then I went to bed and sobbed myself to sleep.

Here, I would like to mention that Cockney funerals were often occasions of ostentation, with plenty of show but always ruled by the purse. Some folks would have two mutes at the door of the home of the departed one. Their job was to be silent, look utterly miserable, and then walk behind the hearse. Oh, what customs there were in those days. They seem fantastic by today's conventions. Every mourner had to be in black, which was a must. Even the horses had black plumes on their heads, like guardsmens' bearskin hats. There might also be plumes on top of the hearse. But it all depended on the amount of cash available from the family and payouts from insurance policies.

My mother's funeral, by Cockney standards, was a very simple one. George and I felt very lonely, as if we had lost a friend.

    Afterwards I began to think about what I would do, with no mum or dad. I decided that I would do my schoolwork in earnest, and try to get a job. I managed to get a little work at a grocer's shop, putting up the shutters at night and taking them down in the morning. Most shops had shutters, which were panels of wood placed close together over the shop windows and secured by bolts from the inside. They protected the glass from being broken, by us kids, and the shops being pilfered, which many shops were because of the amount of hunger about. I also started running errands for the lady in the shop, and received wages of one shilling a week. Here I have a confession to make. I was good at mental arithmetic, and I devised a scheme of putting a farthing or ha'penny on the price of the goods that I purchased for her, which added up to a matter of sixpence a week. May I be forgiven for swindling such nice folk? I was not thinking of spending it on sweets; I badly needed some boots.

Chapter 5 – Street life

Soon, in my own small way, I began to feel independent. I began to make good use of my ill-gotten gains. Sometimes I would speculate and buy a ha'penny worth of crackling from the fish shop and bits of batter that fell off the fish while it was frying. At other times, on a cold night when the fish shop was warm with steam everywhere and it was full of customers all shouting at once, I, being very small, could sneak in and remain there for ages, unseen. What a din there was, with people shouting for a ha'penny bit and ha'penny worth of chips, which would be quite a meal in those days. However, if I was spotted and told to leave, I would get my crackling and my mates and I would sit on the pavement outside and eat a huge newspaper full. A fish shop in those days was really a flourishing business with steam pouring out of the doors into the night air. Food was not so hygienic but it was good and nutritious, not like today with all these modern techniques.

On open-day at school, my drawings were always displayed in the top place, my Horse's Head and Head of Queen Victoria were exhibited at the Town Hall, and I was commended by the headmaster.

After passing the highest standard at school three of us boys were selected to help with a sort of welfare service. On a cold, wet morning the kids without boots or shoes were paraded and we had to wash the mud off their feet, and sometimes their faces and necks too. This was a sad task for us and sadder for them because it was cold water; there were no luxuries then. After ablutions the children were asked if they had eaten breakfast. Those who had not would come along with three of us big lads to the Salvation Army Hall. There they were given tickets for a free breakfast, which consisted of a doorstep slice of bread and jam and a mug of cocoa. If I decided to have some breakfast as well it would cost me a farthing. There were similar arrangements for dinners, except we then went to a shop where pea soup, which was delicious, was issued. This actually cost a ha'penny but the School Board paid.

One winter, children without boots were fitted free with hob-nailed boots. When the right fit was obtained the shoemaker had to put an eyelet in the uppers of the boots, so that parents could not pawn their children's boots. Poor kids always had to suffer.

Shops were open from 8.00 a.m. onwards, some until 9 or 10 at night and some stayed open until midnight. If you had some money, you could always get food.

Saturday night was fun for us kids. We would go to the market place, where there was always plenty of excitement around all the stalls. There would be braziers burning, where we could have a warm, and there would be oil flares for the illuminations, which were very smelly things.

Take a walk with me into the market place. First, here is a stall auctioning cheap china. The stallholder always has plenty of banter. Here is a man making peppermint rock, while you wait, using boilers and pans of sugar. What a lovely smell it is. If you have a penny you could buy four ounces. Next, here is a stall of second-hand clothing, with the ladies busy picking and choosing. Now a stall with books and funny comics, six for a penny and they are rather large ones too. Then a butcher's stall. My word, what an auction he is having. Typical prices would be, a leg or shoulder for one-and-six, enough for the family for a weekend, and just right for Saturday night! "Best steak, eight pence a pound. Ordinary good joints, fourpence a pound. Or, maybe ladies, your ol' man would like some stewing, or pudding meat. Only three-ha'pence a pound." It is strange to think that people could still be hungry with all this food around. Now, Saturday night is clear-out night, because there are no refrigerators to keep food fresh. If we wait until 11 or 12 at night the meat will be almost thrown at us. But so much for the raw meat. Here is a shop to make our mouth water, a cooked-meat butchers, with faggots, pease-pudding, boiled pork, saveloys and pigs trotters. What a lovely smell, so tempting and so aggravating because of our empty pockets. We pass on, to a chap making doughnuts with boiling fat and batter.

The price is seven doughnuts for threepence. All the food is wrapped in newspaper and the quality and taste is first class. Who is this? Oh, it is a quack doctor, looking the part and full of cure-alls and wise cracks. He has a gramophone playing, but why the music? Well, he claims to draw teeth out without any pain and for threepence he gets some boy to volunteer and when he starts pulling the kid's teeth, the music is turned up louder to drown out the boy's yells. Next the jellied eel stall, the Cockney's favourite and always flourishing, with jellied or stewed eels and cockles and mussels. Now a man with a barrel organ grinding out songs and, with a nutcracker voice, he sings the latest. What are the words? For a penny you can buy a copy and find out. Perhaps he is singing this:

We all come in the world with nothing
No clothes to wear but bear in mind
When we die all the money we must leave behind
And finish up just the same as we began
Without the slightest doubt
For we all came into world with nothing
So we can't take anything out.

Enough of that let us move on. Costermongers are yelling their lungs out, "Oranges five a penny... apples penny a pound." Bananas are auctioned in bunches of about twelve for sixpence. This is all very cheap by today's prices but not for us in those days. Now a crowded fish shop with everybody shouting their orders, "Give us a penny-bit-and-ha'p'th, mate." There is no queuing anywhere so it is a case of survival of the fittest. Here, again, the fish must be sold out, so prices will fall. Later, fresh herrings might be sold for a penny a plateful of perhaps five or six. Kippers as cheap as four pairs for tuppence. You might be thinking, "How can anyone be hungry?" But believe me, there are plenty of hungry bellies. Now here is a tailor's stall with readymade suits for men, from fifteen shillings. There are shirts for a couple of shillings. Obviously, these were made by sweated labour, by women who earned as little as twelve shillings for a fifty-six hour week. To give you an idea, a postman's wage in those days was eighteen shillings per week. To get twenty-five shillings a week one had to have a really good job.

So, now we must come to it: the pub. Pubs are sordid places with sawdust and litter on the floors. There are plenty of pubs to choose from - too many - and men and women are crowding around the bars getting inebriated for a few coppers. Children are hanging around the doors waiting in vain for their parents. Pub brawls and fights, often gory affairs, are all too common. Sometimes even women can be seen fighting in the streets.

It was all so disgraceful but that was Cockney life in those days. I am apt, at times, to draw a parallel between modern pop-stars, raving and shouting, while the ladies scream their heads off, and the tumult we had in our day, what with the dads shouting, cursing and fighting to the accompaniment of the womenfolk and children screaming. In both senses, it was hysterical.

On a Sunday morning the market would be open and women could be seen drinking in pubs, whilst at the same time preparing their peas, beans or other vegetables, for dinner. At closing time, 3.00 p.m., bedlam would be let loose. Husbands and wives would be rowing because of spoilt dinners, tempers would rise and, eventually, blows exchanged. Meanwhile the kids would have to wait for dinner. The police were always busy and always came in pairs. It sounds as though folks were wild animals. Thank goodness we have now progressed to better times.

A remarkable invention arrived around 1909 known as 'living pictures'. In these, one could see people moving about or ships in angry seas. You could see four short films for a penny but there were no talkies then. The films had captions and a piano would tinkle out appropriate music to suit the picture. The music might be sad, romantic or any other mood the pianist could devise. All the pictures were shown in complete darkness and each reel was wound back by hand, so there was plenty of waiting time. Some places would have electric lighting but gas was the usual. A number of shops were converted into these 'bioscopes', as they were called, and screens were fixed to the inside of the shop windows with rows of wooden forms for seats. It was nice to get out of the cold and when continuous performances were introduced, children would stop in the place for hours, changing seats at times to fool the attendants, who were always on the look-out for 'long-stayers'.

Another interesting development was taking place in transport at that time; electric trams were introduced and ran alongside horse drawn ones. They ran on batteries but breakdowns were so frequent that horses would often come and take over. Things did slowly improve. There were steam buses on the roads as well, and these contraptions had boilers fitted at the back, but at times the top deck passengers would get covered with smuts. No vehicles had any covered top decks and when it rained a waterproof was provided to keep one 'fairly' dry. The lowest fare was ha'penny a mile. Next there was the motorbus, but again this was not all to be desired. One would see motorbuses every half mile, or so, broken down, and riding one was always a matter of having to change buses every-so-often or walking. The tyres were of solid rubber; certainly an improvement on the steel ones, but it still meant a very bumpy ordeal as they rattled over the granite cobbles. This, added to the staccato clatter of horses' hooves, and all the other traffic, the main roads became places of terrible deafening noise. However, electric trams had come to stay and soon became very popular, travelling much faster than horse trams but, like any invention, there were always improvements to be made and various new types would keep being introduced.

To see a motor car was a real novelty with their high seats and no tops, necessitating Arctic style clothing in winter. Cars were too expensive yet for our locality. The old 'horse brakes' which took people for jaunts about eight miles out into the country were supplanted by motor coaches, charabancs, as they were called. Seats on these were arranged so that passengers in front were at driver level and each row of seats would be a little higher, so that the rear passengers were perched very high up. This commencement of a new era in transport was all very exciting. Steamrollers were used for road mending and were compelled to have a man walk in front of them with a red flag, which is of course laughable now.

    At fourteen years of age, I was getting on very well at school and, having passed all standards, was waiting to leave. Some benevolent people had started the Fresh Air Fund. Its aim was to take children to Epping Forest. On fine days some others and I would write out labels and fix them onto the children's coats, or tie them around their necks, in case they strayed. We would be shepherded to the railway station and then off we would go to Loughton and out into the country with farms, fields and forests. Each child was given a pork pie, a couple of cakes and a bottle of pop. Then came our first ride out in an electric tram, which was so quiet and beautiful. There were hardly any houses in the forest and I thought that this must be God's own country. The visit was too short and too soon we were back to our hum-drum life in Plaistow.

Chapter 6 – Working life and learning a trade

In due course, I left school to start out earning my own living and, at the same time, I joined the Young Men's Bible Class. It was led by a barge builder, who was a man I came to admire because he was a real Christian. Whilst at this class I met a chap who, realising that I was in need of a job, found me one at Augeners Ltd., a music publisher in Newgate Street in the City.

Naturally, I was excited. I was an errand boy and maid-of-all-work. I had to light the office fires, clean the windows, and dust and wash a large office floor every day. My working hours were 8.00 a.m. until 7.00 p.m. and to 5.00 p.m. on Saturdays. My wages were seven shillings a week. I was up at 5.30 every day, with my sandwiches, and off to work. For about three miles of the journey I would walk, or steal rides on carts and vans. Then, for the major part of the journey, I would go by tram, which was tuppence return to Aldgate. For lunch I had three-quarters of an hour and a quarter of an hour for tea. All of which was strictly timed. So, how did I budget for the week? Well, one shilling for fares and the rest I gave up at home, where I was given back one-and-sixpence to buy my own clothes. Anything left over was to pay for my riotous living. So, I still had to scrounge here and there.

My family moved to Liverpool Road, in a half-house, where rent was about three shillings a week. But life became intolerable at home. There were constant scenes involving my stepsister who was acting as 'mother'. She neglected my brother and me and we were kept hungry most of the time. We kept our few belongings, our bits and pieces, handy, in case we needed to flee but where could we go? Our health was showing the strain and eventually we were offered a home by my Bible class teacher. Temporarily we had some good food and peace of mind but we felt like a burden to those kind folks. I hope they had their reward. These people were so practical that they found another home for us, where we settled down again but that too was only temporary and eventually we had to return to live with our stepsisters. Then George found me a job at his firm at eight shillings a week, and with no fares. It was quite a rise but what a job! Here is a brief summary: I started at 6.00 a.m. and knocked off at 5.30 p.m. Saturday I worked until 2.00 p.m. and had a half day off. My job was sorting cement and plaster sacks, which I had to shake out and inspect for holes. If they were wet, I would hang them out to dry. This was on an exposed position on a wharf and I got covered in lime and cement and worked in a perpetual fog. My ears and eyes clogged up and my fingers would be raw with constantly handling the rough sacks. How my frail body stood up to this I will never know. One day a week I spent cutting chaff for the horses using a machine operated by the ostler. That was another filthy job, not white dirt this time but black dust, so I was always coughing it up to clear my throat.

My brother George told the boss that I was good at mental arithmetic, and I was moved to a local depot at Canning Town, which was launching some new lines of paint, timber and ironmongery. That was just the job for me. It was a lot cleaner and I had to deal with customers, which meant I could use my education to the full. My wages were now ten shillings a week, which was much better, but bear in mind we had no annual holidays, only the Bank Holidays. Although hard, the work was interesting. Top weekly wages for foremen at that time were about thirty shillings. Carmen were graded according to the size of their horses; a pony driver would receive about fifteen shillings and a carthorse driver around twenty-five. A sack of cement or plaster weighed about two hundredweight and the carmen had to carry those inside for their customers. Beer seemed to be their chief sustenance, that and some bread and cheese.

Well, I was slowly progressing and acquiring an extensive knowledge of drain pipes, timber and bricks, which were mostly pertaining to building of houses. Houses were very cheap to build at that time. To put you in the picture, here are just a few examples of prices, which I have remembered all these years: wallpaper ranged from a penny-ha'penny to fourpence a roll; paint was one-and-nine pence for seven pounds; a bundle of 500 feet of wooden laths cost about two-and-threepence; twenty bushels of sand, a cubic yard, cost four shillings; a two hundredweight sack of cement cost two-and-sixpence and a thousand bricks were thirty shillings.

Now for a change of scene. My Bible class teacher had arranged with other church folk to send me to a convalescent home at Folkestone for two weeks. I had to get permission from my boss. Incidentally, you got no wages while you were off sick. But those good church people provided me with some money to see me through.

When I arrived at Folkestone I saw the sea for the first time. After having lived in the Dockland squalor, I was fascinated and delighted. The residents of the home, all women, made a real fuss of me and seemed to be like a lot of mothers to me. They sat me at the head of the table at meal times, took me out, treated me to a visit to the fairground and took me for rides on a boat. With all this fuss over me, I wondered if I was dreaming, and I was overjoyed. Being the only boy among thirty or more women, young and old, they really spoilt me. In every sense, they were such kind Christian folk. However, I am afraid my enchantment ended all too soon and I left in tears.

When I arrived back home, after my holiday, I found conditions were awful. After the visit to Folkestone sea-fever had got into my veins and I had a burning desire to do something better with my life. But I soon found out that I was too small in stature for the Royal Navy.

I packed a few things in a large red handkerchief, commonly used in those days by workmen to put their sandwiches in, and went down to one of the big boats lying in the docks. It was called the *Highland Laddie*, and it was bound for Argentina. I sneaked up the gangway, and when I told an officer I wanted a job, he laughed at me, saying, "Go home Son, and eat some more pudding." Being thus thwarted I resolved to improve my physique somehow or another. I was a poor specimen to look at but being wiry and strong I was very good at gymnastics. During the winter, I joined the senior gymnasium at the public baths. I was so keen that I was selected for the Borough's team, and received a medal for eighth prize. Fancy me, Little Titch, as I was called, drilling with the elite, all of whom were fine strapping fellows. However, I was not concerned with medals, I was increasing my height and now I was five feet and one inch. I tried to join the Royal Navy again. Again I was rejected. I plodded on with the exercises, doing two hours of gym every evening, and that after a very tiring ten hours of hard work. I was always thankful when Sunday came around.

My brother George and I were not wanted at home, what with my stepsister being such a tomboy and entertaining her boyfriends in the afternoons. There was never a meal ready for us. We became really despondent and felt that we had to do something about it. George made a box at his depot, which would hold all our belongings. Eventually my sister Ella took us in, although she had enough to do with her own family.

At work I became even more knowledgeable in building materials, so much so that the manager was allowed to take a holiday saying to the boss that, with a little extra assistance, I could manage. So, there I was, virtually in charge of the Canning Town Depot, having two men assisting me with the hard work in the yard, while I managed the shop part and I was not seventeen yet. I had to arrange delivery of goods by horse and cart. Brother George visited me every morning and checked my credit and cash takings. Once or twice I could not quite make my figures tally, a little fiddling became necessary, and with a little ingenuity, I was able to keep a balance on my side.

Well, the boss was so pleased with me I got a rise. "Oh boy!" I thought to myself, "At last, I'm getting somewhere – fancy, I'll soon be walking out on monkeys-parade, what with getting twelve shillings a week!" Monkeys-parade took place after the Sunday evening church service when the young men would eye-up the girls.

When George visited me, at my depot, I noticed he was making eyes at a girl working opposite. She was machining girls' frocks and other things and kept looking up and giggling. I thought he was just being silly but no, she was to be his destiny.

He became happy with Alice's companionship. "Ah well", I thought, "George is happy courting but where do I go from here?" I had some male friends of my own age who I larked about with and not always in mischief. Sometimes we would lark with the girls, after having splashed out on half a pound of Allsorts for three-ha'pence and handed them round.

George smartened up his appearance. He bought a new bowler hat for half a crown and gave me his old one, it being too small for him. My goodness, I felt a real somebody and it boosted my morale. On rare occasions I went to the local music hall. The seats were tuppence, threepence, fourpence or sixpence. There was no queuing in those days, so, an hour-and-a-half before the doors opened, I would line up at the entrance. As the crowds assembled little me used to get jostled away from the door. But when the doors opened everyone surged in and I felt I was being crushed to death. All in an attempt to get the cheapest tuppenny seats. Inside it was always rowdy, unless something sentimental was on. Having some good laughs made a break, though, and it was all great fun. They were far better turns in those days, although they were poorly paid. There was always plenty of melodrama and tear-jerking stuff, which the audience applauded and cheered in real Cockney fashion. If the audience did not like a turn, the act was hooked off the stage with a long pole. An artiste's life was a real uphill struggle because they had to earn their stardom.

When holidays came around the following year the manager had fixed the dates for his holiday, forgetting whether I would stand in for him or not. I told him that unless I got three days holiday I would not take over. He became worried, and it was arranged that I would have my three days holiday.

The Naval Recruiting Office was opposite our depot and I used to see the petty officer strutting about. One day, I said to him, "I wish that I was big enough to join up."

"Come inside", he said, "and let me size you up." I did, and at the end of it he said, "You are only just the five feet three inches and your chest is a little under what it should be but I think we could soon fill you out."

Chapter 7 – 1913 Joining the Navy

So, during my three-day holiday, on July 13th 1913, a day I will never forget, I joined the Royal Navy. In my heart I hated the idea of being in water but not on water. Now a new life started for me and I was very keen.

When I broke the news to my folks, my brother George was very pleased and hoped I would be happy, whilst Ella, my sister, cried about it, but my mind was made up.

Full of wonderment, I went to Chatham barracks and was overawed with all the smartness and discipline. I learned about all the, 'pictures on the wall', as all orders and rules were called and, after the medical check-up, I went to the barrack room, which quartered 192 men. The room was spotlessly clean with all the utensils polished. I was served out with a hammock. Of course, this was something new to me. It was a thick canvas sheet about six feet by four, which was eyeletted at each end to receive cords. These terminated in metal rings, to which was attached thicker ropes for suspension from the two hooks about seven feet above the deck. *Deck* was the new name for the floor. A horsehair bed, about five feet long, went inside the hammock and then a blanket. A pillow would be improvised by any article of clothing, until some kind soul would make one for me. On the first night, when the lads turned in, the fun began. We had to jump up to a bar, raise our legs, sit in the hammock and then let go the bar. If the hammock was not adjusted correctly, out of bed one would tumble and onto the deck five feet below. The deck was wooden and perhaps you can imagine the rumpus as first one, then another, new recruit fell from their hammocks. The only one laughing, though, was the instructor, who would then put us right. Once safely in the contraption I lay and reflected on the old saying, "You've made your bed; now lie on it."

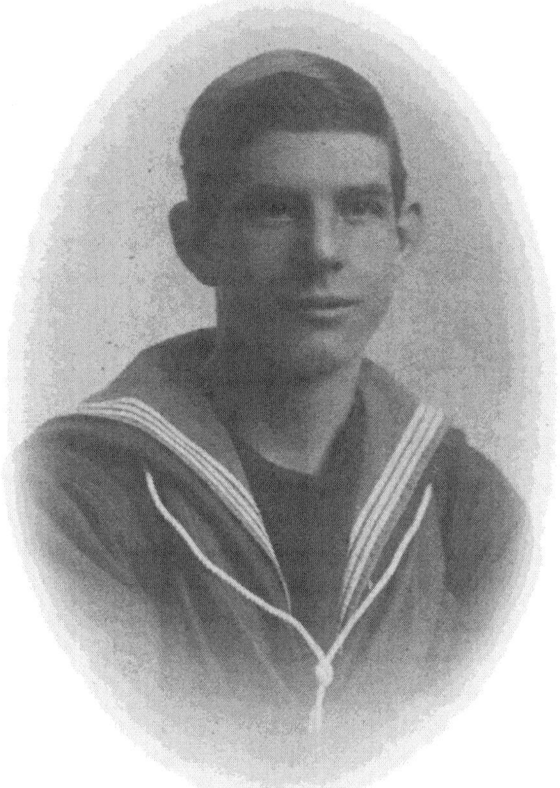

What was I thinking about? Maybe my new role in this young life of mine. After the bugle had sounded 'lights out', the room was darkened and all had to be quiet. We were treated like a lot of children.

Reveille was six in the morning and we were awoken by petty officers shouting, "Wakey, Wakey! Lash up and stew!" If we lagged behind a little, we would be tipped out of bed – Sorry, I mean hammock. Being keen, I jumped out. By the way we had no pyjamas and slept in our flannel vests. There were no cups, so we had a basin of cocoa, which was thick stuff and very nourishing. At that time we were waited upon. Then our hammocks had to be lashed up by rolling them in a long sausage like bundles and, with a lashing rope, turned evenly around them, so it was like a steam roly-poly pudding. We were taught how to lash them properly and were told that, if necessary, they could keep us afloat at sea for quite a long time. Hammocks were stowed away in bins until night time. Next we were detailed for odd jobs of washing and scrubbing places like the landings, washrooms and corridors. All of which had to be done by hand.

I soon learned that we had to be thorough. Two lads would go to the galley, the cookhouse, and gather the breakfast for sixteen men. They would apportion the quantities of food, whatever there was for breakfast, such as sausages, corned beef, salmon fish cakes, eggs and sometimes bacon. All of which were quite nice. For me it was a great hunk of bread, a lump of margarine and tea. Breakfast would be devoured with not a crumb to spare. Remember some of the 'new entries', as we were called, only joined the Royal Navy because they were hungry, and at the end of their tether. Few seemed to have joined for patriotism.

We were in civvies until then, but for our first parade we were kitted out as bluejackets. It was exciting with all the different types of clothing. There was a Sunday best suit with gold badges, which was called N° 1, then our N° 2s, which had red badges. Working suits were of white duck or superfine canvas, with no blue collar and were called N° 5s. We had very thick trousers, as thick as two new blankets, for boiler room work, called N° 6s, which also absorbed the heat from furnaces or steam and lessened the risk of burns. Then there were towels, vests, pants, lanyards and a canvas box with a brass label that had 'F.W.Smith' sewed onto it. This made up a hefty load. Oh, and I forgot, there was the Ditty Box, which you kept your knick-knacks in, such as pen and ink, pencils, stationery and photos of loved ones. But, to start with, I had none of these. In the clothing store the petty officer would look at you, size you up, and sling the items at you, which usually fitted not too badly. We were given a woodcut with our name, and every item had to be stamped. Something to put in my Ditty Box.

We then had to dress up, which was quite a performance, and I was beginning to think how funny I must look. Somehow, perhaps because of my pale face, I did not look the part. I thought I looked ridiculous and anyone could have seen that I was certainly a new entry. After our full issue we stood with our kit bags, while we were arranged into 'messes'. This meant that there were sixteen men at one table, each table bore a number, and that would be our new home. Kitbags were stowed in receptacles showing our nameplate on the bottom.

Without fail, we always had 'pea-do' at dinnertime. This was thick pea soup with plenty of celery seed in it. I loved it and would even like some today. If possible, I would have two helpings, in case the main dish was not very nice but usually the main dish was very good. We had roasts, stews, meat pie and vegetables, which I thought was all good wholesome food, but maybe I just did not know any better.

Dinnertime was something to be seen to be believed, with everybody rushing to get the biggest dinner. This resulted in fights galore, like a lot of wild animals. If one was late, it was just too bad because you got no grub. After a while some order was made and the barrack room was kept clear until all dinners were served out on the table and the 'hounds' were let loose. "Oh my goodness", I thought, "have I got to put up with all this?" You see, no one trusted anybody else. Washing up, and all the chores, had to be done by ourselves, thus making us self reliant, which in later years has always kept me in good stead. After dinner was cleared away and messes made shipshape, we mustered to have our clothes, or kit, marked. Everything had to be marked to prevent thieving.

Shore leave was piped after tea, and that always created a stir. There was the usual rush for victuals, men would grab their portion of bread and put it in their kit bag. Then they would press the margarine on top of their head, while they rushed around cleaning up as much food as they could get. After that, they would scrape the marge from their hair, spread it on their bread and eat it. All these capers, while we were training, were teething troubles, and wore off in time. In other words sanity eventually prevailed and the gluttons were made to look mean and were given punishments to match. The Navy knew very well how to overcome the belligerent type.

Having no money, when others went out, I stayed 'on board'. 'Aboard' being how we referred to the barracks. I would stroll around to see places, like the drill shed, the parade ground, the gymnasium and the swimming baths. Usually my ultimate destination was the canteen, where one could purchase various items like postcards of warships or views of the barracks. The reading room was cosy and there were various other sports rooms but I soon found that my favourite place was the gym.

Then, after all the naval rituals of 'sunset' had been completed, I would usually turn in. We soon started training in earnest at the gym. Early in the morning we would be formed into classes, each with an instructor and then marched to the drill shed. We did not use the parade ground at first because we were considered the 'awkward squad'.

I thought that the morning parades were a wonderful sight. They went like this: 8.45 the parade ground would be teeming with officers and men, at 8.55 a bugle would sound 'fall in', which meant everyone would face a tall mast by the officers' block. Next, another bugle would sound the 'still' and everybody, without exception, stood facing the mast. The Royal Marines Band then played God Save the King, while the White Ensign was raised, and then the Marines would march to the tune Life on the Ocean Wave. All would then muster at the saluting base on the parade ground, where a commander, and his retinue, would be waiting for reports from the officers on parade. I suppose the usual muster would be around 2,000 officers and men. Then, at the appropriate word from the commander, everyone sprang to attention, followed by 'off caps', when the padre would say prayers. It was all very reverent. To end with, the band would strike up, officers would shout and bawl and each platoon would march away in a column. The parade was a wonderful sight, and one in which later I would take part. After morning parade each column would march to their various training duties: gunnery, rifle drill or just squad drill, and some would go into the dockyard. Times of day were made known by the ship's bell and the day was divided into four-hour watches as follows:

Middle watch	-	12 midnight to 4.00 a.m.
Morning watch	-	4.00 a.m. to 8.00 a.m.
Forenoon watch	-	8.00 a.m. to noon.
Afternoon watch	-	noon to 4.00 p.m.
Dog watches –		
First Dog watch	-	4.00 p.m. to 6.00 p.m.
Second Dog watch	-	6.00 p.m. to 8.00 p.m.
First watch	-	8.00 p.m. to midnight

The bell would strike for every half hour of each watch, the number of bells increasing by one, every half-hour. That meant the following:

8 bells would sound at:
4.00 a.m. : 8.00 a.m. : Noon :
4.00 p.m. : Midnight

4 bells would sound at:
6.00 p.m. : 8.00 p.m.
(these being a split watches)

We had squad drill and marching, which I did not mind, as it came easy to me. If some awkward clot misbehaved or showed any slovenliness, we were ordered to 'double', which was a favourite cure for inattention. If the class seemed dull-witted, we would have extra drill after tea, which was not at all nice. But we gradually conformed to discipline, knowing we could not win. With all this rigorous drilling, our smartness and posture improved quite soon.

Now, much to my horror, we were to start swimming lessons. You see, I could not swim. However, we were all marched to the swimming baths and got into bathing slips. This was the first time I had worn any. Then we were lined up on the edge of the pool and as our names were called out we had to jump into the deep end. If we chose, we could dive in. It was ten feet deep. I tried to dodge out of sight because I had butterflies in my tummy and I was scared stiff. I did not know whether to pray or curse. My name was called and I pretended to be deaf. However, I was soon discovered, and, surprisingly to me, the officer was very nice about it and I asked him how to dive in. He told me, and added, "Don't be scared, Son, we'll fish you out." That seemed rather cold comfort to me. My heart kept pounding away with real fear and then I thought, "Why worry? We have all got to die once." Now for the great moment. I dived. But instead of coming to the surface, I came up under a wooden ladder and blacked out. After they had fished me out and pumped the water out of me, I came to, whilst lying on the side of the pool and the officer said, "You can, go and get dressed now."

"Can I try again, Sir?" I asked,

"Certainly, Son, carry on," said the officer, rather surprised. After he had given me some more 'know-how', in I went again. Strange to say, I came to the surface and opened my eyes but I was three yards from the rail. My arms and legs lashed out in instinct and I reached the side under my own steam. I was puffed out but said to myself, "Good old Smudge, at last you've conquered your fear." I went to tea very happy.

The 'passing out swimming test' was a hundred yards in a duck suit, not feathers, but a white canvas suit and until I had passed that test I was still classed as a non-swimmer. However, there were plenty of us classed as non-swimmers. After some half dozen lessons the officer said to me, "Put on the duck suit, lad."

"I can only do ten yards, Sir," I said.

"Then, that means you'll do a hundred yards, if you have to." So, in I went, with the instructor on the side of the pool. I started towards the shallow end while he was patiently telling me to be calm, breathe steadily and not to get flurried. Believe it or not, I managed to get half way and turn around, but then I suddenly could feel the dragging effect of the suit pulling me lower in the water. The officer told me to breathe through my nose and strike out harder, which was good advice. I continued to labour towards the deep end. But now I was becoming waterlogged and tried to get out, but was told that it was only twenty feet more. With the water up to my mouth, I struggled on and heard the Instructor say, "Well done lad, you've passed your test but keep practising." Was I pleased! I had overcome my greatest fear. But I will tell you, I have never been into a swimming pool since. I get no pleasure out of that pastime because I am what is called, a heavy swimmer, which means I have no fat on my bones to make me buoyant.

Now we come to pay day. My wages were eleven shillings and eight-pence a week. The odd one-shilling-and-eight pence was held back and paid quarterly. We would march single file and address the officer thus: "K.19856. F.W.Smith. Stoker 2nd Class." Then while we held our hats out, the officer would place two half-crowns (a half-crown = two shillings and sixpence) on the top of the cap, not inside. But what about the other five shillings? Well, we were compelled to allot that sum to our next-of-kin for safekeeping and to keep a little in reserve for when we were on leave.

Now, we could go on weekend leave. I travelled to Plaistow to my sister Ella's home, where George was staying. Everyone was pleased to see me in uniform and I was made a real fuss of. I also attracted a lot of attention in the Congregational Church, many of the members were glad I had a steady home at last. I shall always remember those kind understanding folk, they made me feel good inside.

After a pleasant weekend I returned to barracks and resumed training. What I found rather irksome was having to change into suits or, as they said in the Navy, 'nautical rig'. The rig of the day would be 'piped'. I found bell-bottom trousers a boon because there was no need to remove my boots when changing trousers. Every item of kit had to be folded 'navy fashion' to avoid unnecessary creases. Jumpers and trousers had to be turned inside out and trouser legs would have to be folded in a concertina fashion. Believe me, kit inspection would be a real ritual. Anything washable had to be clean and any article that went missing had to be made good out of our own pocket money. By present day prices, clothes were very cheap: socks fourpence a pair, towels five pence each and flannel vests two shillings each, to give a few instances.

Well, having arrived in the barracks on Monday, first it was, "Change to suit to N° 3s". These were blue with a red badge, blue collar and gaiters, and were for field training with a rifle. This lasted until dinnertime, or eight-bells. After dinner, there was a change into white duck suits, for engineering training in the dockyard adjoining barracks. There we had a thorough training in how to 'fire-steam boilers' and learned all about ship's machinery.

Fred in his new naval uniform
with his brother George in Plaistow

Stoking, I found out, was an art. It was not just shovelling coal onto a hungry fire. No, we had to do it scientifically, at regular intervals because waste of fuel was forbidden. We practised with stones instead of coal and had lots of lectures on mechanics and various types of boilers. I was really in my element in a dirty job. Then, back to the barracks at seven-bells, 3.30 p.m., where we were dismissed. At eight-bells 'evening quarters' would be sounded by the bugler and the parade ground would become crowded, just like the morning parade, or 'divisions', as we termed it. Now, 'evening quarters' was another ritual carried out by naval personnel, whether ashore or afloat. Its purpose was to carry out a roll call of crews and to check if anyone was missing, which of course at sea is very important.

After 'evening quarters', we scampered off to tea, still in a rush, as we were yet 'untamed'. After tea, the duty-watch would fall in. This usually meant that, one day in four, we would be detailed for various duties, such as room sentries. These were posted in case of fire or disturbance by the lads being drunk or abusive. I myself dreaded having sentry duty on the first watch, 8.00 p.m. to midnight, especially on pay night. When the canteen closed there would be the usual drunks behaving silly or mad by singing and shouting. It was a time when, if you were a sentry, you would need to be tactful and not too bossy, else you would fall into disfavour and be a marked man. Fortunately, I was able to avoid this sort of thing by being meek or by looking the other way and hoping the duty officer would not come along.

Punishments for the defaulters would be various, usually called 10A in the naval code. They would be such things as 'spud bashing', which was peeling heaps of potatoes and vegetables, or extra drill, all at the double, perhaps stoppage of leave, or you could be called early, at about 5.00 a.m., to run round the cinder track. All very irksome. If the defaulter sulked or malingered their punishment would be prolonged, and the Navy always won. Here is one punishment I thought rather apt, and to the point. If one of the men stayed in his hammock, after 'wakey-wakey' or 'reveille', the officer in charge would say, "Oh, so you love your hammock, well then you can cuddle it for two hours every evening for a week." Then the slacker would have to stand cuddling his hammock, off the ground and in full view of sailors passing to and fro. Of course they were held up to ridicule and this usually tamed that complaint.

When on duty at weekends, church parade was compulsory. There were only two denominations, Roman Catholic and Church of England. Officers and men would parade and march with the Royal Marines Band, which I liked. A service was held in the dockyard church and the sailors would be quiet and angelic and then lustily singing the hymns. After service, we went back to barracks marching to 'Sons of the Sea' or 'Hearts of Oak' and after 'dismissal' we would go back to our messes to do anything we wanted, like: reading, writing, sewing or washing clothes.

Whilst on religion, one of my messmates was a Salvationist and before turning in at night he would kneel down on the deck and say his prayers. This led some ignorant lads to be insulting and throwing things at him until, in desperation, he challenged the thrower of some boots to a fight and, I am sorry to say, he came off second best. He said to me one day, "You seem to be an inoffensive chap, what should I do?"

"Look Matey," I said, "why must you kneel on deck, why not say your prayers in your hammock, I'm sure the Almighty will understand? Be judged by your general behaviour and not by a 'holier than thou' attitude. You must gain their respect, at least that is what I aim to do. But pray by all means, I do." He accepted my idea and we remained friends. This story makes me wonder, what should a solitary believer do against such odds? I wonder, what would you have done?

The weeks, and weeks, of training, followed by shore leave carried on. During the training I spent a lot of time on engines and boilers, to be proficient with them. I thought the more I knew about these subjects, the more able I would be, in an emergency, when perhaps my own life would be at stake. Later on, there were many times when this proved to be the case. After four and a half months of strict discipline and teaching, I passed out in all subjects and obtained the highest mark of VGI, 'Very Good Indeed', and the Navy gave nothing higher than that. Now I was ready for sea and eagerly scanned the 'draft list' at the ship's office. I did not wait long, and soon saw that I was to be drafted to the destroyer *HMS Derwent*.

Chapter 8 – First Posting HMS Derwent

I went to Harwich with three other trainees and on arrival I was taken by launch out to my ship, which was lying with others neatly in a row. And there it was, my first glimpse of the destroyer *HMS Derwent*[d]. I gazed over the sea at my new home.

She was rather an old type of destroyer, small, about 500 tons with a speed of 25 knots but she looked like a fast vessel. I stepped aboard my first ship and saluted the quarterdeck. Saluting the officers' quarters aft is a custom adhered to very strictly, and eventually becomes a habit.

After inspection, I was taken forward to the crew's quarters in the narrow sleek bow and descended to the mess-deck, which accommodated about thirty men, the majority of whom were 'old salts'. I was informed, by my mess caterer that I must pull my weight, or else. The full crew would be sixty plus. This would include able seamen, gunnery and torpedo ratings, a cook, a sickbay attendant, but no doctor, and five officers. Fortunately for me, the *Derwent* was a very happy ship, owing to our captain, who was Commander Berwick Curtis, a fine old sea dog, with a naval type beard. I grew to love and trust him. He was a rough-and-ready gentle man, and a man with whom our crew would go anywhere. Our welfare was his chief concern. Even his wife was kindness itself, to all of us. She might arrive on shore at any time, when we were in harbour, and at a wave from her umbrella our signalman would yell, "Molly ashore! Away dingy!" There was always a rush to get into the boat and row ashore to pick her up. She climbed vertical ladders like a sailor and on arrival on board would serve out packets of cigarettes to the three who had volunteered to man the dingy.

As we lay at our moorings, the ship was lifeless, with no electricity, only candlepower. For warmth, we had little coal

---

[d] Fred's Naval record shows that he Joined HMS Kale, Derwent's sister ship, on 23 November 1913. He appears to have swapped between the two ships. See p. 238

stoves on the mess decks and of course there was the galley, where one could cadge hot water for washing clothes. We could not iron anything, so we used to fold clothing carefully and sleep on them in our hammocks, and in that way we got along.

Now for a little excitement. We were raising steam to do some gunnery practice and torpedo running in the North Sea. I was detailed for, boiler room duty, my first real experience. How would I fare? My word those furnaces! Each boiler would burn twelve hundredweight of coal. At first this had to be fed to the stokers by trimmers, and I was one of them. Armed with an oil lamp, like Aladdin, and a short round nosed shovel, I had to work incessantly from the bunker to the boiler room deck. Bunkers on destroyers were really horrible to work in. They were of various types, and situated on the ship's side nearest the boilers. They were about two feet wide, at their widest, and were interspersed with girders. When necessary, I went in with my lamp, and thought, "How dark and grim," as I kept feeding the coal to the little door, which would be shut in an emergency. As I worked away the atmosphere would become choking and I looked like some blacked-up minstrel, with coal dust everywhere. I became aware of the rolling motion of the ship, which felt a little bit odd and as the ship turned and twisted, so did my tummy. Soon I was being as sick as a dog, but there was always the cry from the petty officer, "More coal, you lazy so and so." And so I toiled on.

After my four-hour watch, I went on deck and had a breath of fresh air. Where were we? I could not see any land. Now I really was, 'all at sea'. What a lot of water but at least it was calm. I went forward and just as I was passing, a gun fired. It was the first time I had heard a gun fire and it really startled me, I nearly jumped out of my skin but as time went on, I soon got used to it. I did not fancy it, but I went down below to have some food and a rest, but it was not long before we steamed back into harbour and tied up to a buoy.

We went to sea every day for a week, after which we had daily exercises such as abandon ship, collision quarters, fire and action stations, and we had a man overboard drill, all of which were very necessary. The Navy was very efficient in these matters, and they carried them out very realistically. When abandon ship was piped, our cat, Dick, would always be the first in the skipper's boat. Everyone would leave the ship in a few minutes. My boat was a collapsible Berthon boat, which unfolded and had a canvas hull. It always leaked and continual baling-out was necessary.

    We had quite a few days sailing in and out of harbour and carrying out various exercises, some of which were at full speed. At these times the ship would throb with the clatter of the stokers' shovels and other equipment, and all the accompanying noises made by the roaring of the air fans forcing draughts into the furnaces. I was learning my work, but I was always sick when we were at sea and at those times I felt sorry for myself. However, once in harbour, I would soon recover. All this and, so far, the sea had been smooth. After that we did a spell of harbour training. Including plenty of physical drill and exercise on the upper deck, and this was very necessary in those cramped conditions. Our mess deck was twenty feet long and fifteen feet wide, tapering to about ten. It accommodated twenty-four stokers with two tables and forms, which were firmly secured to the deck. Then there were the kit lockers, so the deck-to-deck space was only about seven feet. When we all turned in, with our hammocks side by side, it was no wonder that the air became very foul but one does get used to the smells of bodies and breath.

    Now about food. The Navy supplied each man with tea, sugar, cocoa, one pound of bread, half a pound of fresh meat, one pound of potatoes per day, a weekly supply of jam, corned beef and rice, plus fourpence-ha'penny in cash each day. This money was to provide for additional vegetables, baking powder, margarine and the like, which were brought to us from shore on a floating ship we called the canteen boat. A married man was usually the caterer, who, with shrewdness and experience, would purchase bacon, sausages or fish, and other tit-bits, for us. If he exceeded the fourpence-ha'penny per day per man, we would have to pay the extra from our pay. The canteen boat would supply us individually with such things as, boot polish, ink, toothpaste, soda for washing, writing paper, cotton for mending and lots of other odds and ends. Each month we had a large nine inches bar of yellow soap and a pound of leaf tobacco for one shilling per pound, or you could have a tin of cigarette rolling tobacco for tuppence a pound. Pipe smokers would make up their leaves into plugs by a unique naval process interesting to watch but hard to explain.

    We had to prepare our own meals and the old salts soon showed us trainees the ropes of making pastry, puddings and stews. My word my stomach had to take a lot of punishment what with my cooking and a keen urge to be sick every time we were at sea. However, with some tuition from the old 'sweats' we got reasonable meals, and sometimes even bacon or sausages for breakfast, which was a relish indeed. We always saved the dripping from the joints for future use. When we were on fishery patrols, on the Dogger Bank, we would get fish galore from the trawlers, all of which was fresh every day and a real treat for me. This we exchanged for tobacco. If only the sea would be kind to me. "When, oh when, will I get my sea-legs?" I would think. Thank goodness my ship had to go into harbour every two or three days to get coaled. Somehow, I managed in spite of the discomfort

    'Coaling the ship' was also an evolution because the idea was always to try to break our previous record. All hands would participate, except for the captain and the cook. The coal was hoisted from a collier in hundredweight bags and manhandled by us into the bunkers, which was a filthy job, that forced everybody to wear any sort of old clothing. We all looked like pirates rather than bluejackets. Being small built myself, I was always bunker trimmer, or at least one of them. A bunker would have two holes on the main deck where coal would be poured into non-stop. When full to the deck, I would push my way down with my lamp, and shovel it into the gloom below in order to fill the bunker in between the two holes on deck, so we might go to sea with our full complement of coal. Sometimes, when coal was near the top,

I would lie on top of it and use my hands to drag my way out. Then it was a case of clearing up the mess, first by washing down the decks, and then washing me down. What a performance that was? Or should I say, ordeal that was? First, we had no bathroom, we bathed in a sheltered corner on the upper deck with a pail of hot water, if there was any, and if there was a cold wind blowing it was very unpleasant. For some reason, I could not face bathing on the mess deck, funny but perhaps I was modest and shy. However, as time went by I become more daring and did not care. After all we were all the same.

After having a bath we washed our clothes, dobying as we called it. Doing this in a small tub with about three changes of water was difficult. It helped to ease the job if we could use soft water, which we sometimes managed with soda that we scrounged. Clotheslines were hung up in the engine room and had to be watched from time to time. Drying washing on the upper deck was not allowed except when the flagship had signalled 'air bedding'. Then blankets were tied to the mast and other parts of the ship and the whole fleet would carry out the order together.

On one trip to sea, we steamed in company with ten destroyers and went to Granton in the Firth of Forth and I had my first real test of an angry sea. I was a little scared, as well as horribly sick. We seemed to be under the water the whole time and the decks were awash from the heavy rolling and pitching. I stayed put in the boiler room hoping to die. Being utterly fed up, or should I say empty, I felt a poor specimen at that time and was I relieved when we dropped anchor and were on an even keel at last. During our stay there, I visited Edinburgh, Dunfermline, Queensferry and other places. I was beginning to see the world but not in comfort, oh no!

Whilst at Granton I had my first glimpse of our battleships and battle cruisers. My word, what an armada, and to me they were huge. Over a thousand men on each and I thought I was in glorious company. I did feel proud, in the loftiest sense, when I saw them steaming out to sea, either in straight lines, or single line ahead, each ship the exact same distance apart. It was an awe inspiring sight. Would they ever fire angry shots? If so, what an inferno they would make. And this was only part of the Grand Fleet.

After a brief stay in harbour we were off again, in divisions, or fours, to different ports. We went to the Tyne, where we had a run around Jarrow, Newcastle and North and South Shields. There, I saw my first coal mine and watched some big ships being built, which was all very interesting. More about the Tyne later. From there we went to Dundee, Peterhead and Inverness in Cromarty Firth and carried out gunnery and torpedo practice in calm waters. Then, off to sea again, and this time to the Shetland Islands. When we entered Scapa Flow another big fleet was at anchor. There I witnessed the ritual of 'sunset', when every ship's bugler sounded the call and all the crews stood to attention facing their white ensigns, which then would slowly descend the jack staff. It was a silent tribute to that piece of bunting, which was our fighting standard and a sight I will always revere with pride.

We carried out night attacks at sea with the 'big fellers', all without lights, which was sometimes dangerous, as we would have to steam full speed through their lines, whilst trying to torpedo them with dummy heads on the 'tin fish' of course. Normally, torpedoes sink after missing their target but they are an expensive item to expend in peacetime. So a dummy head was fitted on the torpedoes, instead of explosives, and after her run, and with her fuel exhausted, she would float on the surface with a smoke flare showing its position. Night or day it could be recovered. Their size varied from about fifteen to thirty feet long and they were nine, eighteen or twenty-one inches in diameter. They had very intricate engines operated by compressed air of terrific pressure and when launched they could travel at forty knots at about six feet deep. The wake made by propellers can be plainly seen and was a real telltale sign.

Now, Scapa Flow is not a nice place to describe. My impression was that it was dreary and desolate and always seemed cold with a full share of gales. No, not a holiday resort, but it was a safe anchorage. Coaling was often performed on the move. We could only carry 160 tons of coal, unlike our big brothers who could hold 2,000 tons or more. Tactical exercises over, we would then clean up in harbour.

Then we broke away from the Fleet to go on fishery patrol on the Dogger Bank, watching the trawlers hauling in their silver harvest by moonlight, a fascinating sight, with the phosphorescence showing up all night long. We had plenty of fish; only I could not enjoy it, as I was not a real sailor yet and was always feeling sick. I accepted the fact that my tummy was going to be neither calm nor normal.

In the late spring of 1914, there was strong talk of the German scare, which had always been a worry for years before, but now it seemed to be getting serious. We had more frequent exercises at sea, and in mid-summer the whole fleet was ordered to Spithead, by the Isle of Wight, for a Royal Naval Review by His Majesty the King. All old destroyers were allotted an anchorage off Selsey Bill. All in straight lines, for as far as one could see, there was the Grand Fleet at Spithead.

I forgot to mention sailors in those days wore straw hats, like some children wear today. We would wear them only on ceremonial occasions. Maybe you have seen pictures of sailors wearing these childish hats. As the Royal Yacht steamed down the miles of lines we had to render three hearty cheers, timed and rehearsed in the early hours. When the Royal Review ended, the fleet had the order to 'battle stations'. Each squadron, or flotilla, was allotted its rendezvous. These seemed ominous proceedings in view of the looming and critical war situation. I was wondering how I would react in a crisis. Would I be a coward or a failure? Not a happy doubt to have.

By that time, because I had become efficient in the boiler room, I was promoted to first class stoker, with a rise of two shillings and sixpence. In all destroyers, and smaller craft, we were allowed 'hard lying' money of sixpence per day. So, my weekly income would be about seventeen shillings. 'Hard lying' money was a little compensation for the discomforts we suffered, such as sometimes having to sleep on the steel deck, owing to the very cramped conditions.

As I said, the Fleet had dispersed to their 'battle stations' and my flotilla was stationed on the River Tyne. Our berths were the Jarrow Slacks, as they were called. We started our sea patrols in divisions of fours. One patrol would take the north from the Tyne to St Abb's Head in Scotland, while the south patrol would cover the area from the Tyne to Flamborough Head. Steaming near to the coast we had close up views of Scarborough, Whitley Bay and Tynemouth. Sometimes we anchored so close to shore the holidaymakers could see us, close up, in all our grime and dirt. Holidaymakers, in their small boats, were intrigued by our feverish activities. It was in Scarborough on the August bank Holiday Monday that we were signalled 'prepare for action'. Torpedoes were fitted with heads, with about 400 pounds of TNT. Live ammunition was stacked around the guns, we had four twelve pounders, and everything on the upper decks including all the brass work had to be painted black. You see, destroyers were usually in night action and being black they would not be spotted by enemy searchlights so easily. Nothing could be allowed to reflect a light, and even our faces would have to be blacked, although, in my case, there was no need for that because, more or less, I was always black. To protect the men on duty, our hammocks were lashed around the bridge, as protection against shrapnel bursts. Our sleeping companions, our hammocks, were now doing a different job.

Chapter 9 – War, HMS Kale and an injury

War with Germany was declared at midnight on 28th July 1914. Our crew total had been brought up to war strength and from now on we were on active service. No lights were allowed on the upper deck and metal covers, or deadlights, were fitted over the portholes. The only light permissible was a shaded one over our stern to give the following ship our position. We were to work in two watches, four hours on and four off, one hour of which would be lookout duties. It was a case of work, eat and, try to, rest. Forty-eight hours patrol was our limit, then we would be relieved, return to harbour and re-coal the ship, which the off duty watches would have to perform. It was always done in a hurry and created pandemonium, while it lasted. Then we would take in stores, food, oil, and other necessities and, after a few hours rest on an even keel, it was off to sea again.

All lights on the coast had to be put out, including lighthouses. Even the blast furnaces at Middlesborough had to cease working because of their glow on the night sky. Coastguards would be warned if we saw any suspicious lights. After a week or two, the coast was blacked out. We steamed in our patrols, always on watch, but without incident.

Once, while investigating a Swedish steamer, we somehow managed to ram her, head on, the impact knocking quite a lot of the crew flat on their backs. Our bows were smashed, so we had to steam to the Tyne. We were hopeful of getting some leave whilst in dock but, oh no, the ship builders worked day and night for four or five days to repair us. The incessant noise of the riveters made conditions such that nobody could sleep and we were glad, ironically, to be under way on our patrol again.

It was thought, by the Navy, that the Germans might be laying mines in the sea-lanes around the coast. So, it came about, on one very dark night near Flamborough Head, having steamed a little out of our normal area, that a lookout reported seeing a red light on the starboard bow, which means about 40 degrees to the right from our course. *HMS Ouse* was ordered by our captain to

Fred's Naval record shows that he Joined HMS Kale, Derwent's sister ship, on 23 November 1913. The two ships were in the same squadron and Fred appears to have swapped between them.

investigate. She increased speed and gave chase. Suddenly, the *Ouse* signalled that she had run ashore, and being very dark, because of the blackout, we had to wait. When dawn broke the red light disappeared and we realised what had happened. We had been off Redcar beach, and it seemed that as the trams approached the seafront and turned to proceed along the promenade, their red rear lights could be seen at sea. The destroyer had chased one of these trams which had turned to go inland. The result being that the *Ouse* had nearly caught the tram... only the beach was in the way. What a laugh we all had. One could hear the officers on their loudhailers expressing their wise cracks in naval jargon. Not for tender ears. However, after dismantling guns and heavy equipment we were able, at flood tide, to drag her off, what the public ashore thought about this incident I dread to think. After that we proceeded on our routine patrol.

As winter approached, and the weather worsened, I was beginning to feel the strain. My stomach was always in revolt and the lack of food was having its effect. The ship's rolling and pitching seemed perpetual. I was utterly dejected and wished myself dead, hoping some wave would end my misery, which only those with a similar experience can understand. One particularly bad night in December there was a northeasterly gale blowing and it was snowing. We seemed to be ploughing under the surface with the ship listing to 15 degrees. Lifelines were rigged on the upper deck for our personal safety because the rails on the side of the ship had been taken away when we cleared for torpedo action. Gun crews, officers and men on the bridge were soaked and freezing. Below decks there was seawater swishing all over the place, not a homely touch at all.

However, it was my turn of duty for six hours in the boiler room, 2.00 until 8.00 a.m. "At least", I thought, "I will be warm! If I can get there." In the darkness I watched the seas flooding the upper deck and crept amidships holding tight to the lifeline. A wave overwhelmed me but I hung on and arrived at the hatch soaked and a little frightened. I was also winded and I clutched for the hatch, which was a circular opening with a straight ladder down to the boiler room deck. As I opened the hatch, the draught from below blew it open. I just got inside when another wave caught me and the rush of seawater went below. How I shut that hatch I will never know. I paused to get my breath and I am afraid I let go a flow of naval blasphemy and I felt a lot better getting that off my chest.

When I landed on the boiler room deck I found that the chief stoker was in charge. This was an unusual event and I wondered why. I was soon to learn the reason. My greeting from him was, "Come here you lazy so-and-so and clear the fires on B1 boiler." I checked my reply which would have been insubordinate and just said, "Aye, aye Chief." My fellow stokers offered to do my stint because I looked so poorly but chief said, "Let that so-and-so do his own work," a remark which stung me. I felt mad. I was finding it hard enough to keep on my feet apart from feeling fed up and sick but then I thought, "I'll show him, I'm not lazy." I will try to describe to you what that job of cleaning the fire was like: the area of the furnace was about six feet by six and the fire had to be nine inches in depth with coal being fed through four furnace doors. The tool used in the operation was a 'slice', which was about nine feet long, and weighed fifty to sixty pounds. This I used first to break the clinker from the fire bars. Another stoker held the door open and held me by the waist, and remember, all the time the ship was rolling badly and I was in a bad temper. I rammed the slice in and out of the furnace for about ten minutes.

The fire I was cleaning was about four hundredweight of white-hot coals, made fiercer by the forced draught. Having done the slicing, then I had to rake the four hundredweight of clinker out onto the deck. Whilst doing that, another stoker had the fresh coal handy and, as the fiery stuff fell at my feet, he had a hose ready to drench it. You can imagine the smoke and steam. Having cleared the fire bars I proceeded with a shovel to put four hundredweight of 'green coal' in the furnace and spread it evenly. Then I raked some live coal on top of this and closed the door, leaving the draught to get it going. I was offered help by the others but Chiefy said, "No, let him be."

So, I filled the clinker and ashes into bags for disposal overboard. But I had not finished yet. In order to clear the front of the boiler, I had to empty the ash pit, at deck level. I took a breather under the fan, which was whirling overhead. It cooled me down but not my temper. "Get on with it!" bellowed ChiefY. So, I continued to rake the ashes out. Now my head had to be very low, about nine inches from the deck, to be able to see what I was doing. My mates were still holding my belt, to steady me but suddenly I was pitched headlong onto the deck by the rolling ship. Muttering sweet words to myself, I got up and carried on. I raked out about a hundredweight of ashes and then filled the ash pit with about two inches of water to keep the fire bars from getting red hot. After that I put the ashes into bags. "Right, you can have a rest now, Sonny Boy," Chiefy said, "but you haven't finished yet."

Funnily enough, all that time, I had not felt seasick and was feeling quite pleased with myself. But I still had to dump those ashes, and that meant going on deck. I braced myself for the task and climbed up onto the deck. With a bowline around my waist and lashed to a torpedo tube, I pulled a bag of ashes up and just tipped them over the upper deck, letting the sea wash them away. Holding on tight, I pulled up all the ashes. I had to work hard because of the biting wind, made all the worse because I had just come up from the inferno below. Then, after what seemed like an endless job, I had finished and went below. After one and a half hours of torture, both mind and body, Chiefy came up to me with a smile on his face, patted me on the back, "Well done lad," he said, "if you want to vent your feelings now, let go." Then he added, "Listen, this is an order: you are now off watch, get forward, have a sluice, drink plenty of ship's cocoa and have some bread and marge. Then get your head down in some snug corner and rest 'til I see you again. Off you go!"

I thought it strange at first but later realised how wise that old sea dog was. He gave me my sea legs, and after that I was able to join in with the rhythm of the ship. I felt like a real Jack Tar from then on. I had a wash, which was a laughable performance when I think back. The weather being so rough, I got half a bucket of hot water, half was enough otherwise it spilt, and then I lashed it, so it didn't move, got my feet straddled firmly over the bucket and removed the grime. As you can imagine the water was black by the time I had finished, which was no matter. Then I dried myself. You see, we were always dirty until we reached harbour, where we could then have a stand up bath on the upper deck, and be screened by a bit of canvas. This was it; life on the ocean waves. After a wash I followed Chiefy's order, had some cocoa and bread and got my head down.

I must have got in Chiefy's good books after that, as I was moved to the engine room for the next trip, working amidst a mass of moving machinery of about 8,000 horse power, and all very interesting. At top speed the engines would turn the propeller shaft at 250 revolutions a minute. My duty was to feel the bearings and to notice, by touch, if any were over-heating, which did happen frequently, and if they were, then to lubricate them or take some other appropriate action. One had to acquire a knack of feeling engine bearings as they flashed up and down. One slip and there would be a serious injury, so I was always careful, especially until I became expert. We used olive oil for lubricating high-speed bearings and engine room hands would be soaked with the stuff, but that was quite a change from coal dust.

I would also take a turn with the evaporating plant, used for converting seawater into freshwater, which was then fed to the boilers. No acid or alkali was allowed to go into the boilers. In fact, if the water remained slightly salty, we had to have it for culinary use, in our tea and the like, which was a flat taste and not very nice. But, in time, one gets used to many things. The water tanks on the mess decks were sometimes locked and the water rationed. One pint per man, per day, for drinking, or for making tea and cocoa. Any tea left in the teapot would be used for shaving. Safety razors had not being invented at that time. But anyway, I did not shave at sea, not with a cutthroat razor, not until later.

Whilst we are visiting the mess deck, let me explain a few things. Tables were secured to the deck by chain fasteners and around the edge of the tabletop there was a beading of one a half inches to prevent food sliding off. We only had basins for tea and soup, which would fit, alongside the plates, in specially designed cabinets. Cups were not a lower deck luxury. Seats of forms were also chained to the deck and clothes lockers were arranged around the side of the ship. For warmth, in harbour, we had a small coal stove on the mess deck, where the smoke could go through a chimney to the upper deck but when at sea a sea-plate was screwed into the flue, making the deck watertight. Then we had no fire. At sea, the mess-deck, with all the portholes closed, was always unsavoury. In fact it was horrible. You see, we had only an eighteen inch round hatch. So, ventilation was nil and the smell of seawater, human breath and bodies... well it was nauseating.

We had an exciting spasm one morning at about 7.00 a.m., or six bells, when we went to 'action stations'. Seawards there had been spotted three German battle cruisers. But then what could we have done against such odds? Their twelve inch guns against our twelve pounders. But as they neared the coast we were ordered by the commander in chief to retire from any action, no doubt our battle fleet were closing in on them, but we were between them and land. The Germans went full speed and opened fire on the towns of Scarborough, Hartlepool and Whitby but they did not stay for long. They were scared, I suppose, of what would happen once we knew of their presence. One of my division's destroyers was sprayed with shrapnel resulting in a couple of lads killed and several other casualties. So, we were ordered to our base, while the big chase went on. However, a sea mist helped the enemy to escape. You see, we had no aircraft then to help in spotting. It was a surprise attack, and was never repeated.

Well, having been at sea for over four months we had to go into dock because our boilers, machinery, propeller, hull, and underwater fittings all needed overhauling. The boilers had to be scoured and cleaned and the main engines attended to.

I had not touched land for four months and wondered what walking on terra firma would be like. The crews were given four days leave to go home. Oh dear, what a 'to-do' that was. I went on leave without a bath and our clothes were not exactly smart. So, I tied up my 'dirties' and hoped my sister Ella would help me out. From Newcastle we went to Kings Cross and then dispersed to our homes.

My arrival and homecoming at my sister's was a special occasion because I was made such a fuss of. This was very strange for me but I loved it very much and had a feeling that someone now cared. Maybe I felt proud because everybody seemed to love sailors. They were all touching my 'dicky' collar for luck, or so they would say. The time flew too fast and I had to return to duty but with all my clothes nice and clean and I had had a good scrub up. I took my leave of the folks at home and returned to join my ship.

The ensuing months were uneventful patrolling up and down the coast, in awful weather at times, but I had got my sea legs at last and I was thankful for that. Now I was a real 'destroyer man' and able to cope. One night in a howling gale, I was on watch in the engine room when someone shouted, "What about some Ki, who'll volunteer?" Ki is what we called cocoa. I said, "I'll go."

"Sure you can manage, Smudge?" said the artificer, "It's rough up topside. Use the life line." So, up I went, got forward and then with the necessary milk, sugar and cocoa, went to the galley with the 'fanny', our slang for a billycan, I was wet through but no matter. Remember the ship was blacked when I crept into the galley, which was a very small place with only room for one man by the stove, but there was somebody already there, in front of the glowing fire.

Fred's nephews and niece, Horrie, Sis and Jack Rogers –dressed in a sailor's suit to welcome Fred home.

"Shove over mate," I said, "let's get in and make some *ki*." The 'somebody' moved and I got in, whilst humming some ditty to myself, when I heard a cultured voice say,

"Could I have a drop of your ki?"

"Yes mate," I said and looked down to see a peaked cap with oak leaves around it. I realised that it was the skipper, down from the bridge for a warm, sitting on his heels, in front of the fire. He was a lovely specimen of a sea dog and a man I looked up to. In fact, the whole crew loved him. He was a daredevil as well, but we trusted him implicitly. His wife was more than generous to me and my shipmates by providing us with comforts and food whenever we made port. She was always there and we adored her too.

The weather was awful that winter, with heavy gales and it was very cold. I remember approaching the river Tyne in a howling gale, the breakwaters invisible, with only the lighthouses showing above the angry sea. We had to steam between these lights, and it was a case of hanging on very tight. As we dipped into a huge wave the deck would be underwater, some water even getting down the funnel and into the boiler rooms, a hazard often experienced in northern waters. Also, it was always a case of leaning forwards, backwards or sideways to try and maintain one's balance. Also care had to be exercised to use the coal in equal quantities from the side bunkers, in case the ship developed a list which cannot be detected while rolling and pitching, until one gets into calmer waters. What a relief it was as we steamed through the breakwaters and got on an even keel. Yes, when in the mood, the sea really was cruel. It is no wonder that sea-faring men are anything but saints, and swear and curse to vent their feelings. We carried on our regular patrolling of the coast, which was uneventful except for the bad weather.

I had been transferred to our sister ship the *Kale* from the same division and on one trip, aboard her, and whilst off Flamborough Head, a howling nor'easter was blowing and we were more under than above the sea, and more like a submarine than a destroyer. My duty was keeping the dynamo running for the electric power, which is housed in a very small compartment, right aft. I had been imprisoned in this small space for about eighteen hours, when I thought I must go forward to get some food. Opening the circular hatch above my head, I started to climb out. I had got one leg on the main deck and was holding the ladder and I landed with one leg out and one dangling in mid-air. I crashed down and landed with the edge of the hatch cutting into the fork of my legs. I tried to keep a presence of mind and sum up the situation. I knew I had really hurt myself; I could feel blood trickling down my leg. Somehow, I rolled onto the deck, whilst hanging on with one hand and then managed to close the hatch. I paused to recover my breath and fortunately I had my wheel spanner in my belt with which I bashed the engine room hatch, hoping to be heard. I was beginning to feel weaker and it being very dark nobody could see me.

HMS Kale

The gale drowned my voice and I thought what a to-do this is. Suddenly, I realised that I had been heard because the hatch opened and a voice said, "Blimey, Smudge, what's happened? Are you all right? All right, hang on a second Mate, I'll get help." He went below and called the bridge and two seamen were sent to my aid. Somehow they dragged me forward and laid me on a table. But we did not carry a doctor, only an attendant. When he saw the blood he was a bit scared. Anyway, he plugged the wound and bound me up but I was in excruciating pain. The skipper came to see me and said, "Don't worry my lad. We'll soon have you comfortable." The ship steamed with all speed possible to Grimsby, where I was taken on board a hospital ship to spend two months recovering. I had smashed part of my urethra. Unfortunately, or should I say fortunately, that was the end of my destroyer life. I was later transferred to Chatham Barracks and it was goodbye to *HMS Kale* and my colleagues. The destroyers were then needed to escort troopships across the Channel, so my old flotilla were sent to Dover and sad to say both *H.M.S Derwent* and *HMS Kale* were blown up by mines with heavy a loss of life. Maybe I was lucky, I do not know.

Chapter 10 – HMS Jessamine

I was feeling very glum and miserable because the news from home, or rather the folks at home, was not too good. My brother George had joined the Royal Field Artillery and was going to France, where our troops were having an awful time. I had thoughts of us being torn apart and me never seeing him again. There seemed nothing more to live for, so, I volunteered for minesweeping or submarines. Maybe I was crazy but it seemed to be that happiness was not for me. Time passed quickly at Chatham barracks, what with having a few runs up the line. Everywhere one went, there were lots of lads in khaki or navy blue and families were worried about their young men.

I kept up my engineering studies until later in the summer of 1915 when I was draughted to a minesweeper building at the Tyne shipyard. So, with others, I proceeded north and joined *HMS Jessamine*. She was one of the many flower class sloops built for patrolling and minesweeping in the North Atlantic. She had a destroyer's hull, fitted with two 4.7-inch guns and some intricate minesweeping gear. She had a single screw, one set of quadruple expansion engines and four coal-fired boilers, which would be harder work than the *Kale* and *Derwent*. She was shallow draught and, as she was a new type of ship, we wondered how she would behave in bad weather. It was a good job that I now had my sea legs. We had some time to acclimatise ourselves to the machinery and workings of the ship, while the dockyard engineers gave us the know-how. Then came the steam trials, gunnery trials and rolling tests followed by the day when we were finely commissioned.

I was off to sea again and this time in the '*Jessie*'. We had ten days provisions aboard but having no refrigerator our meat and vegetables were liable to deteriorate. After four days our bread was stale as well and had to be supplanted by biscuits.

We left the Tyne and steamed north under sealed orders. We kept to the open sea until we passed Dunscansby Head, where we entered the Pentland Firth, and the weather became filthy, with heavy seas and high winds. This was soon telling on the chaps who were on their first trip at sea. As we secured anything that could move, I was wondering how the *Jessie* would behave. We were a little apprehensive, as it was our maiden voyage.

Fortunately, unlike the destroyer's steel decks we had wooden decks and were able to get a grip with our feet. The angle of the rolling, 20 to 30 degrees, was rather frightening sometimes, and we could only make eight knots an hour. In the rough seas the *Jessie* seemed to delight in lifting her nose at every crest of a wave, diving down into the trough, deluging the upper deck with two or three feet of water and then lifting herself up again, as if to shake the water off. "Well", I thought, "we are here and no one can help us." So I hoped for the best. The Pentland Firth is where the North Sea finishes, and as we passed Cape Wrath and into the North Atlantic there was a real hurricane blowing to greet us. We had no thoughts of the Germans, it seemed our enemy was Nature herself; an enemy whose mastery we can never dispute.

The weather did ease a little as we rolled down the west coast of Scotland into the Irish Sea. We steamed south, passing Rosslare and then veered to the west, still into heavy seas, the like of which I had never seen before. I wondered how many of the lads would be saying, "Oh, how I wish I hadn't joined." Perhaps I was one too. We altered course and came into Queensborough Harbour in Cork, where we found other minesweepers. Apparently, the Germans had laid mines outside the harbour and around the Irish coast. But for now, how nice it was to have a good sleep without being rocked in the cradle of the deep, and also to enjoy a good meal. We 'coaled' the ship and took on more supplies. Our duty was to be singly patrolling the shipping lanes, keeping lookout for submarines, which had torpedoed many ships and some big ones among them. By modern methods, we were antiquated, because we had no detecting apparatus, only our eyes.

Our first Atlantic patrol took us about 200 miles west of Ireland and any ships we met, big or small, we would accompany them through our area handing over to another patrol ship, and so on. This was, of course, always 'weather permitting'. After five days at sea, the bread was finished and any fresh food had been eaten. As for our meat, we were served out with salt pork. Oh dear, how would I tackle that nauseating meal? The smell alone was vile and repulsive and in bad weather my stomach could not face it. So, it was corned beef and biscuit for me. The biscuits required soaking before eating. We had tinned potatoes, the smell of which, made one wish one could not smell. I have heard it said that, "One has to acquire certain tastes." I think that applies to smells too. The closed mess deck's atmosphere was appalling, goodness knows what it was like in Nelson's time, this was bad enough. One way I found to eat the salt pork was with mustard pickles, it did seem to help. For me, this first trip knocked all the glamour out of our life on the ocean waves.

We soon had lost half of our crockery but as we never had our meals together, owing to watch keeping and other duties, it was no hardship, and less washing up. Slowly and surely we settled into our new routine and, as the weather abated a little, we could relax a bit. This, unfortunately, also gave the Germans a chance. The SOS calls would be heard by our wireless operator, which he would pass on. Unless we were assured that another ship was nearer, we would proceed towards the victims. It was monotonous really, and at the end of ten days we steamed into Bantry Bay for coal, fresh provisions and a few hours leave ashore. The mail had arrived and there was a parcel for me. Someone was thinking of me. But who? The address was printed and the postmark was North London. I knew nobody in North London and there was not a note inside. But there was a cake, some rock cakes and cigarettes. It was quite a big parcel. We always shared with our messmates any tasty bits from folks at home. I could not thank the sender and thought how silly they were, but there you are, fools or no fools, I was grateful and it made my day. Somebody, somewhere cared for me.

Unfortunately, the Irish were on the verge of rebellion, so we could not get on friendly terms with them, and they were not at all helpful, but I did manage to see some wonderful scenery at

Berehaven. After two days in harbour, we were off to sea again, patrolling from the Fastnet Rock and out to sea for a hundred miles west. There, I saw big liners racing home to Britain, some of which would never arrive. Our maximum speed was only sixteen knots and we could not keep up with the fastest liners, who would run the gauntlet alone. Our shipyards were working all out building escort vessels to combat the German submarine menace, but at the same time the Germans were increasing their numbers and so our losses at sea increased rapidly. Patrolling in the ocean gave one a terribly lonely feeling, as we spent all day and night wondering anxiously, and all the time on the alert. After ten days our fuel and food would be very low, perhaps it was a good job because it gave us forty-eight hours respite. On our way to Queenstown a merchant ship struck a mine outside the harbour. She started to sink but then remained afloat so her crew returned aboard and we took her in tow with our sweeping nets out forward. She was taken into the Dockyard, whilst we bunkered with coal and took on provisions.

We had strict training in such things, as abandon ship, fire, collision, action stations and man-overboard. These drills we had to perfect otherwise panic might ensue. We then learned that we were to be in company with other minesweepers and together we would sweep a big area of the sea that the liners were using. The liners were warned to keep well out to sea. In company with three other minesweepers, we left harbour and started sweeping, which is not a nice pastime for the nerves. Working in the engine room one was filled with pent-up fear and, until we got used to it, any noise out of the ordinary could easily startle us. The ships would work in pairs, with one pair overlapping the other, so that nearly half a mile could be swept in one operation. Whilst astern, there would be a smaller craft armed with a gun to sink any mines brought to the surface. Sometimes they would be exploded with a thunderous roar and throw up a huge volume of water. The sweep wire was an inch in diameter stretching from the stern of the two sweepers and this wire was kept submerged sufficient to drag the cables attached to the mines which would be eight to ten feet below the surface. This was done by a contrivance called a 'kite', named so owing to its shape. We would sweep at six to eight knots.

    I remember my first experience of a mine whilst in the engine room attending the engines. I heard a terrific bang and the ship seemed to lift her stern causing the engine to race. I wondered if it was our ship, it was too close to be healthy. Well, that was my baptism. I heard other thuds and wallops but they were all at a safe distances. When sweeping for mines, everyone aboard became keyed up and, needless to say, we all had our lifesaving apparatus on and ready to use. We would sweep a lane westwards and, as darkness fell, would haul in our sweeps and repair to harbour for the night. Any frayed wires had to be spliced for use again. This was done during the night hours and was not a pleasant task, considering the weather was very cold, freezing in fact. At dawn, we would start all over again in another area with our appointment with fear. After a few days the area we had swept was declared safe and we resumed patrolling.

Chapter 11 – Rescue of the SS Ausonia

Unhappily, whilst off Kinsale Head one day, a Cunard liner, the *SS Ausonia,* was homeward bound for Liverpool with nurses and other passengers from Canada, when a mine exploded under her stern. We happened to be near at hand and raced to her assistance. As we arrived we could see the passengers getting away in boats with the captain and officers trying to prevent panic. The boats were being lowered crazily so that some people fell out. We closed in, with our lifeboats lowered and their crews ready to help in the rescue. The liner was slowly sinking by the stern but slowly enough for our captain to send over our bluejackets to see what they could do to save the ship. The two parties were able to shore up the bulkheads closing all watertight doors, which fortunately held-out and kept the liner afloat. Our captain hailed her and told the liner's captain he would take off the passengers, but as the lifeboats came alongside it was noticed that a few of the liner's crew had panicked and hid in the bottom of the boats, hoping women's skirts would hide them from view. These men were politely told that they would be shot if they stepped aboard our ship, and they were ordered back onto their own ship. So, under protest, they returned. We then took the liner in tow, whilst a tug steamed towards us from Cork. Another sweeper came up as an escort for us. Towing the liner was a slow job.

What about the passengers? As I have said, we were a small ship and now we were overcrowded. Our fresh food and bread had run out but the nurses were very calm, and were a great help in comforting the other passengers, whilst we wondered what we could do about grub and hot drinks. We made some of the ship's cocoa in galvanised pails and served it in basins because we had no cups. How those girls laughed about that. Us stokers were doing our bit by getting flour and bi-carbonate of soda from our store, and knocking up some pastry, rolling it out with bottles on the mess table and using our plates we made some jam tarts. Our ship's cook was busy doing the cooking, so we all kept the galley busy and the passengers thoroughly enjoyed their food. The important thing was to keep the passengers' minds off the immediate danger of mines and torpedoes. So we cleared the mess deck, put out pails of water, with soap and clean towels, and told the ladies that they could clean-up in private, which they gladly agreed to. And it kept them busy. We had to think of everything, and even toilets had to be arranged. The hours dragged on, and never seeming to end. Then, at dusk we posted an extra lookout because submarines usually attacked when there was less visibility at dusk or dawn. The tug arrived and we handed over the towing of the *SS Ausonia* to her, while we stood guard. The damaged ship was well down at the stern but at least she was on an even keel. We entered Queenstown harbour and disembarked our human cargo. How those nurses hugged and kissed us. It was a lovely thank you!

    A little later, when going ashore for a few hours leave, the nurses met us on the jetty and marched us to a big hotel, where we could have anything we wanted to drink or eat. We felt highly honoured. After all, it was only our duty. The next night the nurses met the other watches on shore leave and feted out the same thanks to them.

    Our next patrol was Cape Clear to Kinsale Head where the *Lusitania* had been sunk some time before we arrived in Irish waters. There was a floating wreath commemorating the spot where she went down with a heavy loss of life. Any suspicious neutral ship had to be stopped and searched, as it was suspected they might be fuelling the U-boats by dropping barrels of oil overboard at known rendezvous. One night, with a heavy swell running, I was awakened to make up an armed crew for one of our boats, the whaler. We were to board a Swedish vessel, a task which the seas made very difficult and it was even harder because we were carrying rifles and other gear. However, we made it, and spent thirty minutes aboard the ship. Our officer, a sub-lieutenant, checked the ship's papers and log, while some of us checked the upper deck and cargo holds, and stood guard on the crew's quarters. In the hold it was very dark and somewhat scary, as I have never seen so many big rats. As it transpired, the ship was homeward bound from the South Atlantic whaling grounds and was loaded with whale oil, to be used in margarine making. Two members of the crew were English, which helped quite a lot with explanations. We had coffee with the crew and one of our officers said he would delay our departure if the two Englishmen had any mail they wanted to post. So they hurriedly wrote letters. We returned to the *Jessie*, rolling a little way off, and then back to our patrol again.

Will this ocean ever be tranquil? Not that it upset my stomach now, because I was passed that, but still there was the discomfort at meal times and it disturbed my rest. That, on top of our very poor food and the monotony of escorting merchantmen. Sometimes the merchant ships steamed on a zigzag course, which made the journey even slower. As the numbers of sunken ships mounted, all sorts of wreckage passed us by, and at times we even saw dead bodies in the sea.

We had letters from home, which, if you read between the lines, told of fears of shortages of food and other essentials. I was pleased that about once a month I continued to receive my anonymous parcels, and still not a trace of the sender. After four months of patrolling and sweeping we went into Haulbowline Dockyard, near Cork, to have our engine overhauled, the boilers cleaned and to take in general stores. Also, I was pleased to say, we were given four days leave in two watches.

We travelled from Queenstown to Rosslare, then by steamer to Fishguard and on to Paddington. It was about a seventeen-hour journey in all. I arrived at my sister's home and, strange to say, I met my brother George, home from France. Both of us really had been roughing it, but it was a wonderful reunion, so why worry? We were home and we enjoyed those few hours. You see, I barely had three days, during which George and his fiancée Alice were visiting her sister Louisa in Camberwell. Girls were not in my thoughts and, in fact, I avoided them as much as I could. Anyway, I went to tea with George at Alice's house, where I was introduced to everyone and made a great fuss of. As I was eating tea, I looked at the homemade cakes and suddenly thought that they were identical in every way to the cakes in my mysterious parcels. I said at the table, "These cakes remind me of someone who will persist in sending me parcels but with no name." When no one was looking I popped one into my jumper pocket. That simple action was to start my romantic life. Time on leave was very short and I had to return to Ireland but I had company to see me off. I met up with my shipmates, with their

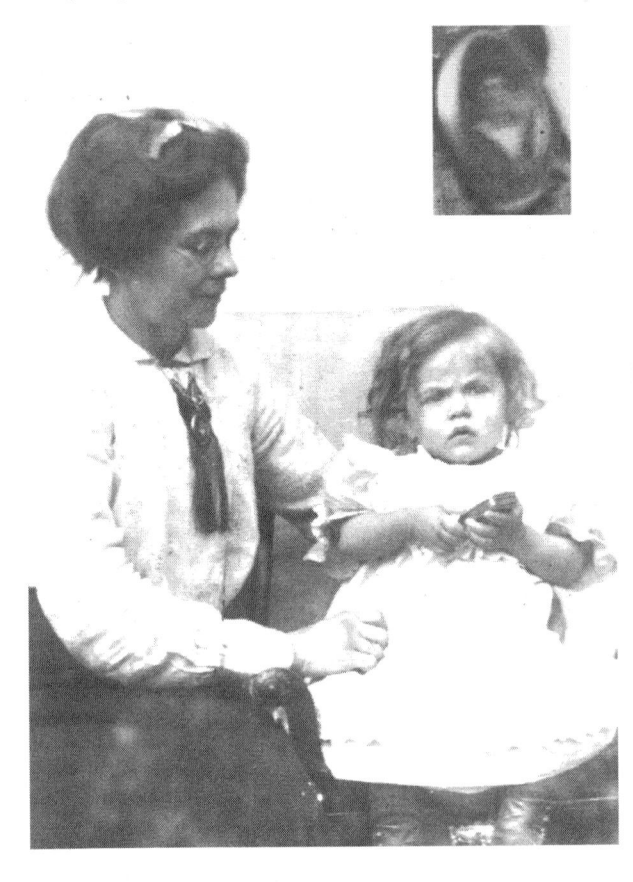

Fred's sister, Ella, wearing a brooch with his picture (inset). The toddler is Ella's fifth child, Emily, born in 1914.

wives and sweethearts. Little did any of us know that some of them would be bereaved in only a few days.

Once aboard ship again, with our repairs completed, we were back on patrol and this time off the coast of Waterford. A heavy swell was running, with mountains of sullen waves, causing us to rise and fall twenty feet from crest to trough, a steady dipping and rolling, which at times was very bad. We could hardly expect to meet a submarine but the weather eased up a lot and in the forenoon we sighted a schooner under half sail. We steamed around her but could see no sign of life. The wheel was lashed in one position and the schooner, the *Cooroy,* was making about six knots. We circled again, this time at 'action stations' with everyone alerted and ready. Our captain decided to board her and investigate. Our whaler with one officer and seven men was lowered within a couple of feet of sea and then dropped a little ahead of *Cooroy.* We dared not stop in case the schooner was a German decoy. The whaler managed to get alongside and a boy seaman was left in the whaler whilst the rest went through the ship's quarters. Then I had a scare; a torpedo was making for us.

    We took evasive action and saw the damned tin-fish glide by our stern missing us by just a few feet. We put on full speed and turned in the direction of the submerged submarine but as we watched the *Cooroy,* she was hit amidships with a mighty roar and disintegrated, going down in less than a minute. She was loaded with iron ore and her bulkheads were pierced which sent her to the bottom quickly. We lowered another boat in case any of our men had survived. It was about a minute later when the vortex had cleared and bits of wreckage floated to the surface that we saw two of our shipmates pop out of the sea. One was the boy, who, in error, had clutched at two oars instead of his boat when the ship had been hit by the torpedo but this had saved his life as they kept him afloat when his whaler was dragged down by the sinking ship. The other, a petty officer who was saved by a life saving waistcoat that his wife had given him. Both were unconscious, and their lungs nearly bursting. While the rescue party was away we steamed and laid a pattern of depth charges hoping we would catch the Jerry sub. Whether we did or not we could not be certain. Wreckage would have helped but the Germans would sometimes discharge oil to fool us. It was a real battle of wits. We picked up our whaler with the two survivors, who we then had to get to hospital. We steamed at full speed for our homeport, having lost six of our small crew, some of whom I had seen at Paddington kissing their loved ones good-bye. I thought how grieved they would be when they knew this truth.

The casualty figures in the news from France were appalling. However, even the strain of that became somewhat accepted by the folks back home. But as the sinking of food ships increased, and made things worse, the hatred of Germans increased in everyone.

In the Royal Navy, if we lost any shipmates, their kit was sold by 'Dutch auction', meaning this: whatever was bid for an article was noted and the highest bidder got the article, but the other bidders paid as well. We would mortgage our pay, so the relatives would have a little ready cash. Relief crewmembers arrived to make up our ship's company and then we were back at sea. The weather worsened and the seas were getting mountainous and made us wonder what good we could do in such conditions. Especially having to steam in total darkness, with our eyes being strained by the constant lookout for other ships. Ah well, that is tenacity of duty. The main deck was continually covered in seawater. It was even washing down the boat deck and pouring down the air vents to the engine and boiler rooms. But we did get sixpence per day for roughing it. Sleep was out of the question and food was all in quick snacks. In the galley, poor old Cookie, apart from being seasick, was often 'put out'. His duty was not to be envied and his language was never intended for tender ears. But more about him later.

There was an incident on one patrol, when I was on watch and stoking the boiler in the aft boiler room. The leading stoker in charge was checking one of the furnaces, which had been gushing out steam and while the furnace door was open the fire was blown out by the force of steam. He ducked but was scalded and burnt. We dragged him away and the trimmer attended him. While warning the engine room to send help, my brain seemed to click into place knowing the danger we were in, of a blow back from the other boilers. I could not see clearly, and knew I had to do something, but what? My training and studying was being put to the test. I clambered on top of the boiler, closed the main valve and opened the safety valve, causing quite a din. Having done that I put the feed pump on full to cool the boiler down. Assistance arrived and a young doctor came down and the injured man was hoisted to the upper deck. In the boiler room visibility was bad, like a very dense fog, and the temperature was rising but fortunately the steam pressure was falling rapidly. I was beginning to feel whacked. I told the engineer officer what I had done but said that the other fires had to be drawn. He said, "All right, lad, you go on deck for a breather and the other lads will do that." So, I went up on deck. To be splashed by the sea coming over the deck was heavenly. But I still felt like a cooked beetroot, with my hands and arms blistered. I went to enquire about the leading stoker and the doctor said he was lucky, as he was well wrapped up with heavy flannel trousers but his back, arms, and head were pretty bad. I had noticed that steam from the safety valve had eased and all the boiler room was under control and I was ordered to rest on my hammock until the doctor attended to me. The next day I had to see the skipper and engineer who questioned me. I was congratulated and, although only two and a half years in service, was promoted to 'acting leading stoker' and took charge of the boiler room. A tender had come out to take the injured man to hospital and, as our speed had been reduced by the incident, we steamed into dock, where the boiler was overhauled.

We were soon put right and, sea worthy again, we set off to sea. As I said before, we were at sea for ten days and in the harbour for two days coaling. At that stage I was watch keeping on the main engines with an artificer and two ratings. My job was tending the various pumps, dynamo engines and condensers. We depended on the machinery for our safety in rough weather, so they could not fail. How we nursed them in very bad weather, pumping out flooding compartments. For example, we had to watch that the main engines did not race when the ship's stern lifted out of the water. That could cause the propeller to thresh the air and the ship be disabled at a critical time. We were always trying to avoid fracturing the propeller shaft, which would render us helpless in a rough sea. At times the engine room would have two or three feet of water in the bilge, that had to be pumped overboard, and sometimes, someone had to strip off and go into the oil and seawater to clean the suction end. He would have to hold his breath and reach through an aperture, where the engines were revolving, and clear the litter to be able to reduce the water level before it got too high. This was a very messy job indeed and so, with the aid of a pail of hot water and a sweat rag, we would take a quick bath.

We all shared the risks, not only me, so do not think that I was out of the ordinary. Oh no, I had many moments of quaking fear. The thing was, to try not to show it. I just do not know how the crews of these vessels stood the test, in the constant vile weather, never on even keel and with lack of sleep or good food. Always it seemed we were soaked, our working shirts would be stiff with salt and we would have to constantly wash them out and dry them on the steam pipes. It became a sort of ritual.

Going off-watch in a fierce gale is something hard to explain in words. Once outside the engine room door, which one always secured tightly, you had to get 'forward' and it seemed that all the forces of nature were against you. Our motto was, "always have one hand on the life line." If the ship rolled your way, then you had to hold on with both hands and let the boiling sea rush by, sometimes up to your waist. It was so black that you could not see anything and the noise was frightening with the wind screaming in your ears. I never rushed and would observe the roll of the ship and the strength of the wind on the weather side. Then, clinging to the lifeline, I would grope my way forward to within five yards of the hatchway to my mess deck, which was in the space below the forecastle at the bow. After *Jessie* had dived into the trough of a wave, she would lift her nose with ten feet of sea crashing into the well space, as the bows lifted again. So one would get through the maelstrom, before *Jessie* dived again. Once on the mess deck, I would begin to get my breath back. But what did I think when I saw my mess mates, some sea sick, others head on arms on the table, and what were they thinking?

Probably their thoughts were of their kin and folks at home, and they would be wondering whether they would see them again. Well, I was thinking too, and very deeply.

I believe in an almighty God for us all but, as to caring for us as individuals, I simply do not believe that. Out there in the Atlantic I wondered, where was that mercy, which was so often talked about in comfortable churches? And what were we receiving at that time, His wrath? If so, it lasted too long and was too unhealthy. In those circumstances it was so hard to be contrite. We certainly felt very humble in that hurricane, but our one consolation was that we were on a seaworthy ship. She rode the sea valiantly and only an error of judgement could render us powerless. So we hoped for the best. What a word *hope* is – when in danger. To be able to write this is a fulfilment of that word.

As the night neared its end and dawn broke, two of us volunteered to brew some tea, as a refresher. It took two men. With the daylight, we left our mess, went on deck, and dodged the seas that were coming inboard. Some of the waves seemed thirty feet above our bows as *Jessie* plunged and lifted her nose high and then, with an almighty "swish", the sea would surge along her main deck. Out of breath, we arrived in the galley and brewed up. Then, lashing the teapot lid on tight, we now had to return to the lads, whilst hoping the salt water did not get in and mix with the tea. We arrived back at the hatchway, soaked but safe. While I held the teapot, the second man held me, and we descended the companion ladder, which was quite a feat. We hung the teapot from a swinging hook and poured our tea into basins. You need an acquired skill to drink from a basin in these conditions without upsetting it down your chest. But the tea helped to relieve our tension. I was on watch at eight bells, or 8.00 a.m., so I had some biscuits and corned beef, and went on duty.

We were recalled and anchored in Bantry Bay for shelter and a brief respite. As we were being re-coaled we were allowed shore leave to purchase some fresh food. We landed at Bere Island, where there were some farms and we purchased some Irish butter and managed to buy a couple of sheep, which one of our crew prepared. We got fresh fish and some bread arrived from Berehaven. The wind had not eased and to see the sea crashing on the rocky seaward side of the bay was awe-inspiring.

Then, after a couple of good night's rest, we were off again, like a policeman on his beat and this time, it seemed that the Atlantic had gone berserk. During the forenoon, the weather was still awful, we were warned to search for one of our sister ships, the *Genista,* which was very similar to the *Jessie*. She was missing from the patrol and supposed to be seventeen miles off our port beam. A zigzag course was planned but, owing to the storm, our speed could not exceed eight knots. On arriving at the rendezvous we searched and searched. Had she foundered in the night? Perhaps. Ships like ours could turn completely over taking all with them. We received no signal from her or found any trace of her. Maybe the *Genista* had had her radio aerial blown away and whilst trying to turn around was caught in one of those huge waves and turned over. We stayed in the vicinity but all to no avail, because we saw nothing at all, not even a buoy or an oar. It gave us a creepy feeling thinking that a ship like ours could disappear. However, and ironically, it made us feel lucky.

We returned to our patrol, with the weather still awful and were all very despondent. One good thing on our side was that we had a well-tried navigator. Navvy, we called him, an officer from the Merchant Navy. Our captain was a lieutenant commander and a deeply religious man, who did not inspire confidence. In fact, we hated him. If he was a Christian, then I was the opposite. He was a tyrant, harsh and without any spark of respect for his crew. I heard the lads saying that they would like to dump him overboard during the night watch, two attempts were made on his life and he was very lucky to get away with it.

One night, in a howling gale, we were hove-to. The engines were doing only eight knots and just keeping our head into the wind, lest we turn over. The fate we feared had befallen the *Genista*. We were all very apprehensive. Then we were told from the bridge that Navvy had taken over the wheel, and that he had ordered the captain to his cabin under 'open arrest'. Navvy, who had not left the bridge for 24 hours, told us that he had to turn the ship around despite the storm and that he would warn us when he was going to turn by blowing the siren. We were to secure everything and hang on to our hammock lashings, as the ship would lurch in the process. So, we waited. Should we pray? Most lads thought praying had been tried before. Some mumbled a prayer for their wives and loved ones, only to end in a blasphemous outburst, as only sailors know how. Then somebody said, "Look lads, let's put our faith in 'Navvy' and trust in him." So, we waited, strained and tense, when a terrific crash and bang came from the bows. We thought we must have hit something. But our port anchor had come loose and fractured the hawse pipe and the chain locker was flooding. The *Jessie* soon became sluggish and not able to lift her bows to the menacing waves.

    Then the ship's siren screamed and I jumped to the alert. My pulse quickened and, as we looked at each other, a voice shouted, "Good luck, Navvy," and I thought, this is it Smudge. The ship rolled over, 25 degrees, maybe more, until she reached the trough in the waves. The sea swept across the main deck, smashing a lifeboat and then entering the air cowls and down into the engine and boiler rooms causing a lot of confusion. With our mess deck now under water, we had no escape. After what seemed an hour, but was probably a few moments, *Jessie* jerked herself back onto her port side and the ferocity of the wind and sea eased. Our Number Two, our Navvy, had done it. "Bravo!" we all shouted. We had to increase our speed; otherwise, the waves would smash the upper deck aft, now that we had the storm on our stern. We were now riding the storm, being helped along by the wind and the waves and with care we could venture on deck. What we had just been through no longer seemed real. Then, our first thought, as ever, a cuppa. Always acceptable.

    The navigator was a blaggard but that night he was an angel to us. If indeed there be such things. We made for land, anywhere would do. Then at dawn we saw the Fastnet Rock lighthouse, and what a welcome sight that was. There, all alone, in the Atlantic enveloped by white foam, but still telling us where we were. After a few hours we were back in Bantry Bay and proceeded to Bantry, and what a pretty little town that seemed. We were on an even keel now and able to assess the damage. It seemed the navigator had gone to the captain and asked him if he was to be disciplined for disobeying his superior officer. The captain said he would let the matter drop. I think the captain was a worried man. Each mess sent a spokesman thanking Navvy for his brilliant seamanship and all he said was, "Look here lads, I was just thinking of my bloody self and while the captain was saying his prayers...well, I had a lucky break. And thank you all for being so calm." That night we could have so easily gone down like the *Genista*. I owe my life to our navigator, of that I am certain. He was a rough type but so human.

We had to wait for calmer weather before proceeding to Queenstown, under escort, as we had two compartments flooded and our engines were not too healthy either. The top of the cylinders were crusted with salt. We ultimately got to the dockyard for some quick repairs and were able to stretch our legs. Unfortunately, ashore the Irish were restive. It was the Sinn Fein rebellion, the Irish were very belligerent, not at all kindly disposed to us and street fights were frequent. But even that was welcomed after our days of uncertainty and hardship.

I remember going to Cork one day and kissing the Blarney Stone, which the legend says is lucky. One ascends a tower and leans over, and another person holds your feet and gently eases you down about three feet to kiss the stone. I would not advise any tubby chaps to try it. Your only luck would be that your mate did not let go of your legs!

Chapter 12 – Minesweeping

Repairs completed and the weather having at last moderated, we were off to sea again and this time for a spell of minesweeping. At that time trawlers were being introduced for the sweeping business. One evening at dusk, I was on watch in the engine room, while a seaman was hauling the sweep wire inboard. We were stopped and could hear the capstan, aft, clanking round and then heard it stop. All the seamen rushed forward shouting, "Look out." Then there was silence. Us engineers wondered what had happened but the bridge piped the order, "All hands but one to leave the engine room and go forward." And we were told to obey the telegraph promptly. The artificer was a nervy character, maybe I was too, but I wanted to take over as he had family and I did not. But no, he would not hear of it, so I kept him company for moral support. Seemingly, a mine was tangled in our sweep wire and dangling about twenty feet from our stern, which was not a comforting thought. One seaman volunteered to reverse the capstan and gently lower the mine back. Down below our engine telegraph rang, 'slow ahead.' I nearly jumped out of my skin, "I know," I said, "For Christ's, sake Jock, do the right thing!" He did, and the mine was slacked away and it dropped clear of the sweep wire. The seaman let the wire go overboard and when we were at a safe distance the mine was blown up by gunfire. That was another little ordeal over. Every day was a hazard but I thought, "I shouldn't grumble. I did volunteer for this, and somebody's got to do it."

Going into harbour each night we were able to get regular mail, and again I received another parcel. "I'll chance it", I thought, "and thank Alice's sister Louisa, for her kindness." That started up our correspondence and was the beginning of our romance.

Fred fourth from right, on his later ship, HMS Ceres.

It was funny, how the tone of our letters slowly became endearing. Each letter brought me a lot of pleasure and a warm feeling that now someone cared for me. You see, I was normally of a shy nature, and I had built up a resistance to the ladies. But I am afraid, or should I say pleased, to say that this correspondence seemed to completely change my outlook on life.

We went back to sea again. This time patrolling in the shipping lanes and hopefully accompanying inward bound ships with their precious cargoes safely home. But losses at sea were still very heavy and there always seemed to be an SOS coming in. The U-boats were getting busier and more elusive but by zigzagging a course, our ships became a more difficult target to hit. Also in bad weather it was thought ships would be safer from U-boats.

Sometimes, in a small, way we were able to help lighthouse crews. It was very hazardous to relieve lighthouses and lightships in the bad weather and they would often be on emergency rations for ages. We would tie a line to an empty barrel, then approach the lightship, drop the barrel and steam round the lightship bows. The lightship's crew would fish up the line with a boat hook as it floated across their bows. Then we could pass a watertight container with newspapers, magazines, tobacco and, if need be, some rough tack of corned beef and biscuits. All of which would be thankfully received. In return, we would haul across some salt fish, which the lightship's crew had caught. One particular light ship, the *Daunt Rock,* off Queenstown harbour, afterwards broke away from her moorings in the heavy seas. In spite of attempts at rescue from lifeboats and coast guards, she was dashed on the coastal rocks and all the crew perished.

Such stories of the sea and its cruel moods sicken one, but our means of survival depend upon the sea, and so we carry on.

One day, whilst on patrol, fifty miles off the west coast of Ireland, we sighted a schooner. We signalled her but there was no reply and, remembering the previous decoy, we approached nearer with depth charges ready and at 'action stations'. As we closed in on her, a seemingly, lifeless seaman was spotted standing against the mast on our side. He was waving with one hand, the other apparently shattered. Our signalman spotted that it was a message. With his one good hand he was sending a Morse code message, using short and long movements, saying, "Don't stop. Sub on Port Beam." That was the side away from us. So, we increased speed and turned in that direction. Things were primitive in those days, with no Asdic listening apparatus to give us a position on a U-boat, and we had to use guesswork. We wove a pattern of depth charges and anxiously waited for any evidence. Perhaps we sank her, but it was very difficult to confirm and we waited ready with our guns, should she surface.

I am afraid that after the treatment we had seen the Germans mete out to our seamen who had crossed their paths, our tempers, and frame of mind, were such that we would not have been merciful. We would have been out for vengeance.

Then we had to rescue the seaman from the schooner, without stopping. We lowered a small boat and he was brought off but he was in poor shape. His left arm was shattered and it had to be amputated by our surgeon. The rest of his crew had been machine gunned by the submarine crew but he had managed to hide by the mast. To tow the schooner would have meant being a sitting target, so our captain decided to sink her by gunfire, a pity, but as a derelict, with no lights, she was a hazard at sea.

On another occasion we were escorting a large liner in a calm sea, when at dusk a thick fog developed. Now this is one of those things to experience at sea. Extra lookouts had to be posted on the bow and stern, and all just listening for the 'big fellow' who we were looking after. At sea a fog can be patchy or it might persist. The sirens blew at regular intervals, and it was like a game of hide-and-seek, with us trying to trace the direction of the liner's siren. We seemed to be keeping in touch, as it were, but nobody could sleep. At 3.00 a.m. the liner seemed close astern, so we increased speed but suddenly her black bows appeared right on our stern. A collision seemed likely, so our depth charges were hurriedly un-shipped. A quick exchange of signals was carried out and we altered course. A cold sweat came over me but slowly and surely we drifted away from her. Phew! What a relief. We parted, temporarily, and made contact again at daybreak.

Chapter 13 – Home leave... and romance blossoms

We handed the liner over and then turned about to meet our next rendezvous, and this time in clear weather. And so we carried on escorting ships until it was time to go into harbour for a refit, which was about every four months and then with our usual four days home leave. What a relief that was and what a pleasure to make personal contact with my 'benefactor'. I was so grateful to her that I hugged and kissed her, oblivious of her friends who were there. 'Miss Bence', Louisa, that was her name, blushed and seemed flabbergasted at my greeting. Any inhibitions that I had towards a lady seemed to vanish and I said to her, "I do hope I have not appeared rash, but I can't express my gratitude in any other way, please excuse me."

"Of course I'll excuse you", Louisa said, "if you'll excuse me." And she returned the compliment. Our eyes were wet with tears, not of sorrow but joy, and for a spell I forgot all my troubles. Need I say about the leg pulling I got? But at that time there was only one person on my mind. I thought to myself, "Smudge, you are slipping." Maybe Louisa felt the same.

Afterwards I learned that Louisa had a similar background to that of mine. Her father had deserted his family through drink and her mother and four children were left without means. I will never know how they managed. Their mother died early, from worry and privation, and Louisa, the eldest, took over. An impossible task for a teenager. But her sister Alice and her brother Alf really suffered because they became separated until her Uncle Matt (Matthew Haswell) came to the rescue and took Louisa and her brother Alf to live with him at Camberwell. Louisa worked as a housekeeper and Alf helped with his poster printing business. Alice got a job as a machinist in Canning Town, which were long hours for very little money. Uncle Matt always made me very welcome at Camberwell.

Above: Ella, George, Alice, Fred, Beatrice, Baby Jessamine, Horace & Ernie – in Plaistow.
Below: Alice, Jessamine and Louisa at First Avenue

Louisa's brother Alf joined the Machine Gun Corps and was in France, where my brother George was suffering privations in the trenches of Flanders. To brighten up my leave a party was made up with some friends and we went to the Globe Theatre and saw a play called 'Romance'. I afterwards thought that it was strange, because it was to begin mine. "Maybe", I thought, "when I return to sea, I might change my mind." but that wasn't to be. Once at sea I received comforting letters expressing care and sorrow for my situation and so my resistance collapsed and I was under a spell of sincere friendship or should I be bold and say *love*, a word I never thought was for me. And so it happened that I was courting by post. It gave me a terrific boost and now I wanted to go on living. I am not sure why I am saying all this now, all these years later, but I hope that perhaps you will understand.

Now, back to the cruel sea. Was it going to snatch my newfound happiness away, or not? After the other half of the crew had had their leave, we started on our monotonous patrols in the heavy Atlantic swell again. These were not white horses but huge walls of grey water. When in the trough it would seem we would be enveloped but *Jessie* would rise and fall perhaps thirty feet. My tummy could take it now and we were all becoming accustomed to this treatment.

One day, we had an ex-railwayman on duty as lookout in the crow's nest. He was a conscientious type and reported to the bridge that he could see a small boat with a signal of distress. All lookouts concentrated in the direction given but nobody else saw anything, except seawater. We altered course to the reported position but after an hour, the captain decided to resume patrol. However, the lookout insisted and pleaded to carry on the search. Well the skipper was reluctant to follow this crazy notion, yet he altered course again and increased speed. The lookout was straining his eyes straight ahead and suddenly shouted, "Boat dead ahead, Sir!" It was not an illusion; it was a ship's lifeboat with five very weak men aboard. We lowered a boat and rowed over to help them. They could not speak because their tongues were stuck to the roof of their mouths with thirst, and they were nearly dead. We thought they might be merchantmen and so asked them which ship they were from. One man tried to speak and we thought he said, "U-5." Could they be Germans? Anger arose amongst some of our ship's crew. They wanted to sink them with their boat. Then someone shouted, "He didn't say 'U-5', he said 'Q-5!'"

"Hang on, I know one of them!" Another of our men said, "They're bluejackets." So we carefully got them aboard and it was noticed that Insurance Cards were in the stern and the remains of their boots, the uppers of which they had been biting for moisture. Once on board the doctor forbade any solid food being given to them, so we heated some tins of Ideal Milk, with some rum in it, and they were nursed like children. Small brushes were used to get their tongues loose. With patience, and us as willing nurses, they gradually improved, and this time, the sea was robbed. Later they unfolded their story of how their ship, the Q-5 had sunk a U-boat.

To revert to the lookout for a moment, this event and his success seemed to have turned his brain and he became incoherent in speech and wild in his actions. Poor chap what a reward for saving five human souls. Soon he did not recognise his shipmates, or the men he had saved, and unfortunately he had to go into a mental institution. What a trick of fate this turned out to be. Another incident over.

I had a new job, which was chiefly on the upper deck with the capstan engines and steering equipment. I was also in charge of checking bunkers, relieving any leading stoker or petty officer and was a storekeeper, in charge of replenishing the engine room with lubricants - for the engines, not the men.

Out upon the ocean one felt completely out of touch with the rest of the world. There were only the daily bulletins of news about the war, and most of them were disheartening.

Our next patrol was fifty miles south-west of the Fastnet Rock, and there we encountered bad weather. To add to our discomfort our engines were giving trouble. To stop and carry out repairs was impossible, so we sought shelter in Bantry Bay, which was a rugged but beautiful spot. Together with some others, I went to Berehaven and to a village called Castletown. Our only transport over the mountains was by donkey and what a laugh that was. The donkeys did not need a guide, because they knew the way and took us. It is true we had sea legs but not sea bottoms. It was quite a change of feelings, but it was great fun. The people were very friendly and we enjoyed our visit to this quaint village. We also came home on donkey-back and afterwards our walking began showing the signs of this bareback riding. But what a lovely change, even if we did walk a bit funny afterwards.

My naval pay in early 1916, even with hard lying money, was not quite a pound a week. From that I had to buy my clothing and any extra food, and so it was difficult to save much cash. The admiralty made no allowance for our generosity towards any scantily clothed shipwreck survivors we picked up. We had to put something on their bodies, and to us it seemed the most natural thing to do. After all, it may have been us in need of human kindness at another time. However, as the numbers of ships being sunk were mounting, it seemed ludicrous to have to rely on kindness or religious conviction to help those suffering. The world seemed crazy.

Answering distress signals was quite a daily affair and mostly we were either too late or someone faster had effected a rescue. Some ships were sunk without trace, and at other times the only evidence was some floating cargo, the dead bodies of people or maybe even the carcases of dead horses. There might be a huge patch of oil, which, although it had the effect of calming the sea, would be dangerous for those trying to survive in it. One such case we came across was that of a small tanker sinking, with her oil cargo drifting around in the heavy swell. Her lifeboats were all smashed, and so while we stood by, her crew had to jump into the sea. We then steamed through the oil, closer to the tanker and put out a sort of raft made of oars and rope, which acted as a kind of floating mat. The seamen were able to clutch at the oars and we could then drag them on board. If any survivors got into difficulty it was a case of one of us volunteering to jump in with a bowline around the waist. They had to clutch hold of the survivor, who could be floating unconscious in their lifejacket, and then the pair would be pulled to our ship's side. Of course, the sea would all the time be doing its best to claim more victims.

On one occasion, when a boat could not be lowered, I did this, giving me a glow of satisfaction to have made a rescue. The heavy rolling of our ship made things more difficult. Once in the water she seemed to surge and tower over me at times. Everyone was desperately trying to cling on. Then eventually when the ship rolled away the poor sailor and I were snatched with a jerk out of the water, leaving us breathless, and, believe me, what a relief it was to feel the strong arms of my shipmates around us. When all were aboard the survivors would often stand, with tears in their eyes, thinking of their lost comrades and watch their ship take its final plunge.

Now we had to get them shipshape. First, we stripped them of any clothing and with hot soapy water removed the muck from their bodies. Oil would take a lot of patience to remove, especially from the hair. While the bathing was going on rum and hot cocoa would be served. Then we had to get them into the warm, wearing our spare dry clothing. Some of us would wash their clothing. Of course this all had to be done by hand. The injured would be in the Doc's care.

Whilst on the long journey back to Queenstown, the rescued would sometimes decide to help us and we would distribute them on watch as lookouts, or give them engine or boiler room duties. I had a lad of sixteen with me in the engine room once. He told me that he had been torpedoed twice before. Later, I learned from his mother, in Wales, that he was torpedoed four times altogether. After that, she kept him at home, "...until he could join the Army," she told me.

During incidents like these, my own personal feelings were at the back of my mind. The bitter cold and the constant soakings did not seem to matter then. It is now, in my old age, I find it hard to imagine how I endured such things, and how anyone endured such things. I will never forget that period in the Atlantic. I still see the scared faces in the mountainous seas. I now find that so difficult to describe and difficult to forgive. In particular it is difficult to forgive Mother Nature for her cruelty to those of us who dared to defy her. We human beings, in our small boats, were defying nature a lot in those days and, seemingly, regardless of our own safety.

After about four days with this extra crew of rescued sailors we would usually land them at Queenstown and after handshakes and hugs they would give three cheers for the *Jessie*. And so we would go back to our monotonous procedure of coaling and taking in stores. Any incident would provide some variety from our routine, and even the trouble ashore, with the Sinn Feiners, who were now becoming more threatening, was a change. What a prospect, when one was expecting a little peace and quiet. Picket duty to supplement the police ashore was imposed on us and we had to be very tactful, or else we could get hurt.

Ashore, it was a real pleasure to have a shave. I am sure we must have looked like pirates, rather than the spick-and-span bluejackets of our barrack days. In spite of our ordeals, strange to say, we kept pretty healthy. Even colds were scarce and my nasal catarrh had, it seemed, gone forever. I was never of a big physique but I was nimble, strong and active (How I wish I was now). Maybe roughing it and living in a primitive way was good for us all. Even the folks at home on short rations and plain food seemed to thrive. It is astonishing what the human body can take.

My story would seem to indicate the weather was always foul, but, oh no, during the summer of 1916 we had some lovely weather. Such weather as holidaymakers would dream of and that made one feel good, and praise Mother Nature rather than curse her.

It was a time to have a good scrub up of our bedding and wash out our blankets. Thank goodness we had no sheets. Also, in the fine weather, we could have more baths on the upper deck. We could sunbathe, keeping a pair of trousers on in case we had to go to 'action stations'.

Writing letters to lady friends was a common past time, and I was fortunate because Louisa corresponded quite often. Her letters certainly did cheer me up. My early experiences of writing to her were so strange, because I did not know which words to use in order that I might express my pleasure. I could not remember hearing words such as *love, dearest* or *darling*, before. Her letters were so full of warm sincerity. Her one desire seemed to be to help me and it would have been caddish of me to be just *matter of fact* in my letters. So, I followed my natural impulse and reciprocated with feelings of love and sincerity. Thus, I became a new person. I was in love and through our letters we grew fonder and fonder. I now had something, and someone, to live for.

How I eagerly awaited the mail, wondering what her reaction would be to my last letter. Now the die was cast and we enjoyed each other's letters, but should she be my fiancée? Whilst the thought made me very happy, it reminded me of the danger I was in. I kept saying to myself, "You mustn't get engaged, Smudge, you might be killed." This, I explained to Louisa and she replied, "Remember, it would be better to have loved and lost than never to have loved at all." Well, this got me thinking and, together with my natural instincts of love, it persuaded me to say, "Yes," to the question in her letter, and we were engaged.

Now we both had to start saving. And there was another laugh. How much a week could I save? Five shillings a week for a year would be thirteen pounds, but one could not do much with that. I remembered an advert which said, "You find the girl and we will find you a home for ten pounds." Then I thought, "Shall I?" This was indeed a financial problem but then I remembered that I should be due for promotion to petty officer soon, and that would help. Louisa, now my fiancée, got a job as a post woman for just under a pound a week. She would be able to save more than me. But more about this later.

We enjoyed the good weather but so did the Germans, who were busy laying mines in the shipping lanes. They especially were keen to place them outside harbours. Cork harbour seemed a favourite spot, and the existence of these mines only became known when ships were blown up.

The captain was a religious maniac who made our life unbearable by his hard discipline, which he kept up, whatever the weather. The crew all hated him and nobody wished to emulate his beliefs. He insisted that 'divine services' were compulsory, so one Sunday morning we were on the upper deck holding our hymnbooks, whilst at same time our ship was sweeping for mines. We were sweeping together with *HMS Mignonette* and two other ships of our class and while prayers were said by our captain, the *Mignonette* struck a mine and blew up killing fourteen men. We had to release the sweep wire, turn to help, and, if possible, save lives, whilst remaining oblivious of our own danger. The next day another sloop, the *Alyssum*, sweeping the same minefield blew up. But luckily all her crew were saved. On board the *Jessie*, we were naturally alarmed by these disasters, but it was a case of carry on until the sweeping of the minefield was completed. Many mines were exploded but I breathed a sigh of relief when evening came and we returned to harbour. "Another of my nine lives gone," I thought. "Will my luck hold out during this war?" The dangers seemed to be getting more intense than ever. Many merchantmen were lost, or crippled, by these dreaded mines. The U-boats would not risk surfacing during the day to recharge batteries and would have to wait until night. It was a battle of wits. The Navy thought they had an answer in their secret Q-ships. They sailed under neutral colours but always the White Ensign would be raised at the critical moment and guns uncovered and fired before the U-boat could submerge. With luck, she would be sent to her doom in minutes. This made the Germans even more artful and their U-boats began to ignore the flags and sink neutral ships as well, assuming that they were all Q-ships.

Another artifice of the Royal Navy was a schooner that would apparently be steadily sailing along, but beneath her she would be towing one of our submarines. The U-boat would close in on the schooner to be able to sink her with gunfire, thus saving on torpedoes. The commander of the schooner, a submarine officer in telephone communication with our submarine, would give the bearings of the U-boat and our submarine would torpedo the U-boat whilst on the surface. Survivors, if any, would be taken prisoner. And so the game was played.

One night we, and some others, had to rendezvous in the Bay of Biscay to pick up a convoy with an armed trawler escort. The speed of a convoy is the speed of its slowest ship. On this occasion there were about twenty or more ships, of all nationalities. At dawn and dusk U-boats could choose their positions without being detected and so vigilance, on our part, was even more necessary. We were making about eight knots on a zigzag course, all the ships keeping to their stations, and the escort ships steaming up and down the lines of vessels. At dusk, one merchantman was lagging astern and signalled that her engines were giving trouble. She drifted further astern on her own and, whilst a sloop was steaming towards her, gunfire was heard. It turned out that she was one of our Q-ships which had caught the U-boat by her artful trick before our sloop could reach the scene. As the Q-ship steamed and caught us up our captain challenged her over the hailer as to her identity. The answer was in nautical terms, which I will not quote. We later learned that it was Captain Campbell VC, a hero of Q-ship warfare. This man would disguise his ship during the night by painting his funnel a different colour and rigging canvas superstructure so as not to be recognised. He had a free hand and would join convoys during darkness and then leave when action demanded it. With a lot of luck that particular convoy arrived safe and sound. We left them off Falmouth for our destroyers to take over, and we returned to Ireland.

Every cargo was a vital necessity at home, where they were dependent on our merchantmen. Already people were tightening their belts. Casualties in France were mounting and thousands were being killed. Not a street in Britain was left without bereavement. It appeared to be being accepted with calm, yet sad, composure. However, every family dreaded the postman. Yet people carried on with their work. Even working harder to avenge their loved ones. It is funny how calamities and misfortunes can knit together a brotherhood of man, which is a thing religion has never managed to do. However, sympathy and kindness will soon be forgotten in peacetime, when selfishness and greed will again take over. "What a pity", I think. But such is the truth of man's affairs.

Chapter 14 – Engagement rings and trouble in Ireland

It was late summer in 1916 and I had another four days leave and spent most of that time at Camberwell, with Louisa, my fiancée, and it gave us time to get to know each other better. She bought me a signet ring from a pawnshop. It had to be a cheap one, but in fact I am still wearing it today, after fifty years. What stories it could tell. It is a reminder of the loyalty and sacrifice of someone so very dear to me.

At times when I am alone, I love to be nostalgic and think of Louisa's devotion to me, of our struggle together through strenuous times and to remember us both thinking of each other's welfare. I hope I repaid her love with interest.

In exchange for my ring, I bought her an engagement ring. I had to borrow some money to get it, but no matter. She demurred, thinking she was too old for me but then she consented.

My brother George, whilst on leave from France and a few weeks before I had arrived home on leave, had married Louisa's sister, Alice. Two brothers marrying two sisters. I was a little late for George's wedding but we had quite a celebration. I wondered how I would shape up to being married. It would be quite a problem with so little cash. Also I was wondering if I had done the sensible thing, knowing what was still before me. Winter was on its way and I would be in the Atlantic again.

Whenever I wrote to Louisa, I did not quote my plight or hardships. What was the use anyway, why alarm everybody? They all had enough trouble to contend with. However, even then, I think Louisa knew. Our affection grew stronger, which gave us both something to live for, and to hope for. Again that word *hope* was uppermost in my thoughts. When we parted at Paddington, I was sad at heart and so was she, but both of us were trying hard to suppress our feelings. Louisa tried to smile as she clung to me but there were tears. Fortunately Uncle Matt was there and then one of my shipmates shouted, "Come on Smudge!" What could I do? I will never forget that moment of saying farewell. "Cheerio my dear," I said, "God bless you." Louisa plucked up courage, smiled, waved goodbye and I joined my shipmates. What a horrible journey back, and first few days in Ireland, that was, until I got the usual reassuring letter and parcel. Returning on board, the other half of the ship's company went on their leave. I was able to go ashore once or twice and noticed a lot of Marines and Highlanders around. Apparently they were being given a rest from fighting in France, but their real purpose was to keep order in the town because of the Sinn Feiner riots. Any men in uniform were jeered at and insulted, resulting in fighting in the streets and pubs. I did not frequent pubs, I only went ashore to stretch my legs and have some good walks with a pal or two. Besides I was nearly broke, a very common occurrence, and I was trying to save but became resigned to being hard up. The ordinary soldier's pay was only seven shillings a week, and so it would be a few weeks before the Highlanders could cut-loose, as it were. Mind you, beer was very cheap compared to today's prices; only tuppence a pint and cigarettes were a penny for five, or posh ones, tuppence-ha'penny for ten. A cup of tea cost a penny, and there were places, especially at ports, where a cuppa was free. It was nice to land at Rosslare harbour at about 4 a.m., after a bad crossing of the Irish Sea, to be greeted at the bottom of the gangway by Irish colleens with a stall of steaming cups of tea. Wherever we went, at any hour, no matter the weather, there were ladies with cups of tea. How we blessed those ladies, "Bless 'em all!" says I.

 One evening ashore I was in charge of a picket, which consisted of two other stokers and me. Pickets had been doubled, so I knew trouble was expected. My beat was on the main street, where there were plenty of pubs and, being evening time, they were very rowdy. The Irish constabulary was out in force and kept very busy but we only had to deal with naval misconduct. Our picket was not armed, and just had leather belts, canvas gaiters, whistles and an armlet with NP on it, standing for Navy police. I warned my chaps that, as it was near closing time, we could expect insults from civilians but should ignore them, and try to get locals to keep their tempers. We should not ask for more trouble as there seemed to be plenty quite rife already. As we reached the end of our beat, we heard another patrol's whistle calling for help. Of course, we could not ignore that, and so went towards the scene of the trouble. There was a crowd of about fifty or sixty men and women, in the middle of which was our patrol under attack. I ordered my two chaps to hide their belts and armlets, and pull trousers over gaiters, so as not to appear authoritative and we pushed our way to the centre of the crowd, where the patrol leader was lying in the road injured and unconscious. Then a bluejacket and marine arrived, so I now had four men with me. I received a few clouts, and a lot of abuse, as we pushed open a space amid all the shouting. I whistled for assistance and attended to the man on the ground, who was bleeding and lay quite still. As I rose to look around to see if help was coming, I was struck on the head with something hard, I was bleeding and felt as if I would pass out. But I am afraid it put me in a fearful temper. Then a chap pointed out the young woman who had hit me. She had a bottle in a string bag. As a last resort, and to break up the party, I ordered, "Swing the buckles of your belts!" As my men swung their belts, so the pressure eased, and then help arrived and I could seize the young woman who had struck me. We arrested her, and some of the more belligerent characters, and frog-marched them off. We even had to drag some of them over the cobblestones, making their knees bleed, in order to get them to the guardhouse and be able to hand them over to the civilian police. We then thanked the Tommies for rescuing us. "Quite a restful evening, all in all," I thought.

 Time to go back to sea again. It was late autumn, so we expected bad weather and, sure enough, it was waiting to rock us to sleep. When we left harbour we heard that we would no longer be sweeping for mines, which we thought was quite a relief. Trawlers and drifters, escorted by destroyers, were to take our place. Destroyers could go twice as fast as us, at about thirty-four knots. From now on we would be in full swing on convoy work.

There were still heavy losses, and thousands of tons of good food went to the bottom of the sea, which seemed a dreadful waste. To watch those gallant ships make their final plunge to the bottom of the sea, whilst knowing that some poor living soul was still on board, and without hope, was all very poignant.

At least with convoys we would have plenty of company in case of trouble. However, the Germans were becoming very audacious; it was our cunning against their audaciousness.

A submarine would dare not show itself and use its guns by day and had to wait until night to charge its batteries. Of course, we had no aircraft in those days and so our effectiveness was limited. The U-boats were not having things easy either and their losses were heavy. One reason for this was our Q-ships, which were manned by bluejackets. They dressed as merchantmen, and sometimes even women passengers. At close quarters they would even pretend to panic in order to hoodwink the Germans, and to give themselves time to aim their hidden guns at the U-boat. These Q-boats were becoming very successful.

For us it was convoy after convoy, which was a very monotonous job but we always had to be on the alert, never easing our watch over those grey waters. To try and save ships and cargo, lame ducks were escorted to the nearest dock. One such ship that we escorted into dock was well down in the water and she had a list. Once in dock, volunteers were wanted at night to recover the bodies from below decks, and I went with a party with shovels to empty their bunkers by shovelling the coal through the hole made by the tin-fish. It was rather an eerie job, because sometimes one found a human leg or arm. When my shovel struck flesh it gave me a terrible feeling of wanting to be sick. We gathered the remains of what had been men, and buried them in a communal grave. I thought, "There but for the Grace of God, go I." But this was war, and sentimentality was supposed to be out of the question.

And so we returned to sea to renew our struggle against a ferocious enemy. Our whole crew was infused with two purposes, revenge and pity. Pity went with an offer of help for the victims, which is a common code these days.

Any festive days, such as Christmas or Easter, we would pass like any other. Their significance would be totally submerged, sometimes in monotony and sometime in strenuous days battling against the enemy and the elements. Someday, I hoped, these lost days would be returned to me. But now, I must tell you about our ship's cook.

The cook's galley was about seven feet by five, with a coal-burning range, kettle steamers and large saucepans. In very heavy seas his fire was often put out by pans spilling over and, if he was using frying fat, it might spill and catch light. Everything on top of the stove had to be secured by steel bars. The galley being battened down and its skylight closed, you can imagine the atmosphere was awful in there. And then there was the cook's language, which was hilariously cockney most of the time. At times, I thought the cook would go crazy because his conditions were enough to try the patience of a saint. His platitudes would be shocking, making even our sailors blush. He would put a meat pie in the oven and it would come out, oosh, which is Navy slang for stew, or it might end up like stewed steak because the crust had slithered off in the oven, and if that happened the oven would emit volumes of smoke. I find it difficult to describe the conditions this cook endured. Sometimes his hair was matted with the fat and he looked like a chimney sweep, and if the ship reeled heavily he was often thrown to the floor, and since that was also greasy he would slide around. Thank goodness he knew how to hold on. As I have already described, one sailor from each mess would have to undertake the ordeal of fetching the food from the galley and returning it to his mess deck. The cook's panic would only last about two hours, but that was long enough. No wonder he would be glad when we were back on bully beef and biscuits again.

As we continued escorting ships, we looked forward to our next spell in the dockyard for refitting, when we could have a good wash and brush up and look human again. We might also get the chance of a four day break.

In writing my letters home, any mention of marriage arrangements seemed ludicrous, as my circumstances were so bad, but we did plan, which perhaps took our minds off the affairs of the day.

Home leave eventually arrived and I was off home again. Need I say how we met? War was forgotten for a few hours, we did not worry each other with our troubles, especially about cash, which was always a problem – and always will be I think. Uncle Matt was very generous in lots of ways, not wanting us to feel 'out of the times' as it were, and somehow that gave us a little pride. The fighting men were always at a disadvantage compared to the men who stopped at home and earned good money. But despite not being able to stand my corner, I was always treated well. This inequality in values of service rendered will always puzzle me. At home, the folks comfortable beds, food and pleasures, were barred to us lads trying our best to get that food across the seas and to their homes. And at what a cost! No, I did not feel a mumper. It was just that I did not have money to spill like the workers did at home, who could even go on strike, whilst we had to grin and bear it. Oh well, that is life, I suppose.

Louisa and I discussed getting married and weighed up the pros and cons. My money was about eighteen shillings a week and I would be entitled to a marriage allowance of a further six shillings a week. She was a post-woman earning perhaps twenty-five shillings a week. We thought we could just about get along on that and so decided to go ahead. However, we had no dreams of a posh home. But then, neither of us had ever had a comfortable home of our own. One room would do, at least while the war lasted, but that seemed as if it might be forever. I left all the arrangements to her, because I knew she would cope better than me, so motherly in her understanding and always putting me on a pedestal.

I thought that our parting this time would be really upsetting and I dreaded it, but then her brother, Alf, came home unexpectedly from the trenches and that took our minds off our own problems. What a pitiful sight he looked, with Flanders mud all over his uniform. He would not go indoors until he had had a wash down and a change of clothes, so everybody got busy. What a game that was. I was with him outside in the shed and he said, "Fred, I'm lousy, I can't go in." So, I helped him scrub down with carbolic soap and put his clothing in soak. He was healthy enough and so pleased to be in clean clothes and soon his sisters Alice and Louisa were hugging him to death, and half crying and half laughing. I washed out his clothes for him and then joined the party. The girls were baking cakes and Uncle Matt was buying some drinks. We made it a real party.

I had quite a few to see me off at Paddington and Alf being there helped a lot to ease my departure. I often look back to those farewells at Paddington, with each pair of parting couples centred on each other and oblivious to all the other activities taking place around them. There would be troops arriving and departing and the wounded returning from the front with nurses and ambulance staff. It was all very busy.

It was 'hail and farewell' to London and my loved ones and back to *Jessie*, hoping she might behave kindly as she should in the heavy seas. But I trusted her; and to have faith in one's own ship gives one added confidence.

If I appear to be a sentimentalist, I do not mind, because it is a human trait of mine and I like people to know it. Maybe the human race would be kinder to each other with a little more sentimentality.

Chapter 15 – Rescue of SS California and a wedding!

Here we go once again, back to the cruel sea, always there waiting for those who challenge it. Tuned up engines, plenty of stores taken on board and we were off for another twelve days and nights. The weather at that time of year, December 1916, was not the sort you would pick for a pleasure cruise, but by then the *Jessie* was a good old timer, and, so long as she was handled right, she would ride the waves with ease. We received plenty of SOS calls for help but for most of those we were eventually not needed, or we were too late. It was always disappointing to reach a rendezvous only to find nothing but a vast expanse of green rollers. The ship may have sunk, steamed away or perhaps we had been given the wrong position.

It was a day in February when we were steaming head-on, through a real snorter of a gale, when we received a call from the liner *S.S. California*, which was urgently requiring assistance because she was sinking. She was only about thirty miles away, so we made all the speed we dare. Full speed was not possible lest the seas smash our upper deck. We heard that the sinking liner had a few hundred passengers on board and that more ships were on the way. We prepared rafts, as our boats would be of no use in the rough seas. It was bitterly cold and the screaming wind seem to shout at us in defiance. It was dark when we reached the vicinity where the ship should have been but she had already disappeared. All sorts of wreckage was crashing over our bows. Barrels and cases were splitting open and strewing their contents over the decks, and we even saw dead horses. As we eased down our speed all eyes were fixed on our small search light playing over the water. Then we saw some survivors in life jackets and with our rafts we were able to pull quite a number on board, while other ships began to arrive and pick up many others.

A woman's long hair was seen amidst the foam and one of our lads jumped in quite close to her with a line. The sailor signalled that he needed help, so another stoker jumped in, and me being a lightweight did as well. She was a young woman with two young children clinging to her. She was all but gone, so we parted her from the children and signalled 'heave away'. We were then dragged alongside our ship and as the *Jessie* rolled away, we were jerked out of the sea towards the deck. Then the *Jessie* rolled back towards us and for a moment it seemed as though she would turn over on top of us. Then after another huge wave, and another jerk, we were hauled aboard. I was holding a child clear of the ship's side by turning my back to the hull and the rivets and thought that I was unhurt apart from being winded, but once aboard, the salt water got into my cuts and my raw flesh and it was very painful. It all seemed to last for hours but in fact it was only a few minutes.

Now we had to revive these people and take stock, while everybody else was busy rescuing as many of the others as they could. The women were scantily clad; some in just nightdresses, and their long hair was all matted with oil. We had a job on hand but once we got them below, although crowded, they were in the warm and, at least for the time being, safe. Hot cocoa and rum were served out and to keep the children quiet, and to cheer them up, some jam was emptied in a basin with a big spoon and served with some softened ships biscuits. Some of the lads made pastry and jam tarts came to the rescue once again, because, of course, we had no bread left. Some of the rescued did not rally and others sobbed because they had lost someone, and there were children who may have lost their parents. Who had been saved? We could not say until all the rescue ships had reached harbour.

All thoughts of modesty had to be put aside, as our aim was to get them warm, fed and clean. The emphasis was on *clean*, as some were in a dreadful condition. The mess deck was in a terrible state as well, owing to the pitching and tossing of the ship. The passengers were too wrapped up in their thoughts to smile but we did our best to cheer them up and reassure them. Many were violently seasick and only our crew were allowed on upper deck to empty buckets. We screened off part of the mess deck with blankets for the ladies' toilet but some were very weak and needing help. It was organised chaos but at least we did our best to get them comfortable.

I spoke to the young woman with the two children, who I had assisted; one of the children was her own and the other had lost her mother but the woman had taken both into her care. She rallied very quickly and was surprised to find she was wearing a flannel vest and 'duck pants' and that her long hair was clean. She raised a smile and a "thank you." Others would take over looking after our passengers, when we went on watch. The weather had eased a little during the night allowing us to put on speed, and, as was the case with all the other recue ships, we steamed for Queenstown.

Food had to be improvised with soaked biscuits, which were very hard, bully beef, pickles, salmon and rice puddings, which our guests appreciated. It kept them going and some were able to help in looking after each other's needs. Their cuts and abrasions were treated and some managed to get some sleep. After a couple of days of this we crept into harbour where ambulances, cars, and doctors were waiting. We assisted them down the gangway, the ladies blowing kisses and the men shaking our hands. And that was another episode over.

I thought, "What a crazy world we live in, when women and children are subjected to this inhuman behaviour on the part of the enemy. Where is the sense in all of this?" I think there were 186 saved that night but many were lost forever. It was a pity that the sea could not have been kinder. Prayers seemed a mockery and my belief was shaken. I shall never understand the working of 'destiny', because it appears so hard and cruel.

I suppose I ought to count my blessings; quite a lot of sloops were either sunk or disabled but our *Jessie* would crawl into harbour time and again, and although sometimes her engines were groaning for urgent attention, she would pull through.

And so the weeks rolled on. My letters were telling me that our marriage had been arranged for my next leave. It would have to be a floating date, as I could not know when I would get shore leave. An officer gave me a hint that leave would be in early

March. So I made arrangements and at home plans were hatched. We were to live in the cottage at Camberwell and share Uncle Matt's home, so only the bare necessities were needed. I could muster about five pounds and my messmates bought us a honeycomb quilt for a present.

As we were going into dock, I applied to the captain for two back-to-back leaves. A mate had volunteered to be a substitute. However, our pious captain refused straightaway, saying, "Don't you know there's a war on? What's more, you'd be on second leave when the ship's under sailing orders, and that just wouldn't do!" I was flabbergasted and disgusted but the navigator sent for me and told me to go ahead with my plans, and that he would see that I got away. I was to get ready for the only train that day and stay out of sight until the leave boat left with the captain aboard. Then the navigator had a boat lowered, bundled me in and wished me good luck, but he warned me to keep out of sight of the captain, who, by the way, was a commander by then. I got my free railway pass, my leave ticket and, with a bundle of washing, off I went. The navigator had signalled ashore to delay the train for me, and as I approached the barrier furtively, the ticket collector was hurrying everyone on, so I went at the double and was out of breath by the time I jumped in a compartment with some of my crewmates.

The captain made the rounds on the train, in case of rowdy conduct, so I feigned sleep, with my cap over my eyes. I had to stay on the alert for the entire seventeen-hour journey to Paddington. There was no one to meet me at the station, so I went straight to the cottage in Camberwell and what a welcome I received. Although the date of my homecoming had been doubtful, as soon as I arrived, I settled in fine. But when I saw all the grub for the guests, my heart sank. It looked lovely but I was thinking how little cash I had. I need not have been concerned, because the wedding feast was paid for by Uncle Matt and some other friends, whom I did not even know.

We were married on the 4th March 1917 at the Emmanuel church in Camberwell. And did I have butterflies in my tummy?

However, everything worked out wonderfully. We started off with just a kitchen table, a bed, household linen and other little items. We had no chairs, and used Uncle Matt's furniture. I was in a whirl, wondering how I would cope, because I hated feeling the poor relation, but Louisa, my wife, reassured me that all would come out right in the end and that all the bills would be met. Uncle's friends were all working on newspapers and had money to burn. It seemed all those who stayed at home were in the money, whilst those in the forces were only getting a few shillings a week. To treat a serviceman was thought to be a magnanimous gesture, but I had other views.

These few days on terra firma were a blessing and I was able to enjoy good food without spilling it all over myself. I felt that I had landed in a new world. I was being made a fuss of, had someone to care for me, and I was no longer on my own. I only hoped that I would one day repay my dear wife for her kindness and her love; something I thought was never for me.

After this enjoyable spell, I went back to duty with the usual sad leave-taking at Paddington station. I asked for no tears, just a simple departure, until we met again. Life at that time seemed all speculation, with no certainties. "After all", I thought, "I am only one of millions doing their duty in this war. "That was not exactly a comforting thought but at least I was not alone.

I had my leg pulled when I got back on board and reported to the navigator that all had gone well and that there had been no 'incidents'. I gave him a piece of wedding cake and a big thank you for his generous action. We all put our faith in that man, even if he was a blaggard to the Navy, to us he was a saint and we all respected and admired him.

By the spring of 1917 the war was hotting up again, although we were continuing to improve in our techniques of combating the U-boats and mines. 'Travelling in convoy' was the order of the day and supplies from the USA were now flooding into the country. The Irish were still troublesome and necessitating troops being retained to keep order and there had to be a constant watch kept on the coastline, especially the West Coast, as it was thought enemy agents were busy there, but that is another story.

On our next patrol we were cruising among the Skellig islands, just off the Killarney coast, a hazardous job and made more so because we steamed without lights, in order to be able to intercept any U-boats that might try and contact their spies ashore. The weather was good on this trip, a pleasure cruise by day, with some rugged scenery, as any map will show. Time marched on as we working to a strict pattern and routine. Vast areas were under surveillance and now we had a new addition to boost our forces. The Americans had entered the war, which brought a sigh a relief everywhere amongst the allies. They sent forty destroyers, some of which were stationed with us at Queenstown. The Americans shared some of our sea duties, and our pleasures ashore, so we soon made friends with them. In bad weather they would make for shelter, while we had to stick it out, apparently, our sloops could take it. Their ships seemed a bit frail, often getting their upper decks smashed but they soon got used to the duties. Their stay at sea was far shorter than ours but they did liven up our monotony ashore by purchasing a swimming bath and converting it into a huge canteen and cinema with beds. We were made welcome and the food was delicious and very cheap. Improvised bands with banjos and guitars made a wonderful change of atmosphere. In spite of the Sinn Feiners, shore leave was indeed something to look forward to. Our own Admiralty never did things like that.

The summer months passed by with nothing out of the ordinary happening at sea. This gave us a breathing space before the dreaded winter arrived. But in August I had another few days of leave coming up, and now I had a wife waiting in our lovely welcoming home. Thanks to my lucky stars, I was able to make it, even if it was for only three days. My brief stay was very cosy and homely and I had a wonderful feeling of being wanted and loved. Even if we did not have much money, we were very happy indeed. We had our usual family get together, in the form of a party with a second hand piano in the cottage. That was the first time I started to tinkle out tunes on the piano. We had some good talent among our friends. Uncle Matt and some others sang songs and we had a good party. It was not like these days, when everything is laid on for you. We went to a posh cinema at the Elephant and Castle, where the seats were threepence each. At the matinee this included a cup of tea and biscuits thrown in. The tram fares to the cinema were only a ha'penny a mile and it was a frequent service. But all good times come to an end, and so I returned to *Jessie*. It is funny how sailors have affection for their ships. For a lot of the time ships are subjected to their sailors' curses but in reality they always love them. Possibly, this is like a landlubber loves his home, which is just as they should.

My period with *Jessie* was nearly at an end; usually one serves about two years in one ship. But, in the meantime, off we went with the Yanks to keep us company. They had more speed than we did, and so our convoys could be larger, with fewer losses, whilst the German U-boat losses mounted.

During the summer I was able to swot up for my engineering 'knowledge', with the help of my engineer officer. I managed to keep a clean record with my work, which meant that I soon had an examination paper to answer from the Admiralty. It had rather a lot of questions about boilers, engines and auxiliary machinery, all of which I answered in full detail. I put all I knew into that examination for petty officer but I thought, being only twenty-three years old, I was probably too young. Three other men were given tests and they had double my service, but I passed with flying colours, whilst the others failed. So, I then had to await my orders from Chatham. My home on *Jessie* was nearing its end and I wondered what would be in store for me.

We entered the winter season with trepidation and fear; will our luck hold out? We soon started pitching and rolling, which is something one has to endure to understand. Sailors will say that each gale they encounter is the worst in living memory but I cannot say because they all seemed bad to me. I remember my last Atlantic week of bad weather. After three days of maddening wind of high velocity, we lost a young seaman one night. He left the wireless cabin with a message to take to the bridge, which was only about five yards but he never arrived and must have been blown off the ladder up to the bridge and fell overboard. He was not missed until the possibility of his rescue had long past. We also developed other troubles; a gun broke loose, which was secured but only with great difficulty; one of the ship's boats was stove in; a boiler was put out of action and, worst of all, our engines were not working properly. After my mates and I had been nursing the engines and pumps, at eight bells, midnight, I went off watch. As I stepped out of the engine room, I suddenly realised a storm shutter had been swept away and at each roll of the ship, the sea was rushing through and onto the main deck. I had not long to decide what to do. But as I clung to the guardrail in the darkness I was swept off my feet, the water forcing me to let go of my grip and sweeping me aft. I groped wildly for a handhold and it seemed an eternity before my hands grabbed a wire stay. As the ship rolled over and the sea subsided, I was left dangling in mid air and wondering where I was. Then again the sea came on board and as I swung with the roll, my feet touched something around which I twined my legs as tight as I could.

While I got my breath back, I sensed I was caught in the rigging of the after masts. I edged myself slowly down, whilst trying to keep a firm grip, until I felt the gunwale of the ship. I was only about three feet from help on the main deck but it was no use shouting. I had to hang on through each roll of the ship, which swept me in waist-deep seawater. But then I knew exactly where I was. I had about four yards to cover before the life rail and so I waited for a suitable roll of the ship, and clambered along to the engine room door, where I joined my watch, hoped for daylight and decided to stay put; I could not be relieved anyway. Was I thankful! Fifty years later, I now realise that if I had missed that rigging that night, I would not be writing this story.

Our wireless aerial had been blown away, the wind and sea had upset our position and our speed had been reduced so much that we were actually going astern. So, once again our hero, Navvy, turned us around and eased the situation. Before daybreak, we were challenged by some harbour guns and found ourselves in Milford Haven, which is a long way from Waterford. At last we had a lull and whilst at anchor, and waiting for the gale to blow itself out, we made *Jessie* seaworthy again. The old girl had done it again!

I have often relived that night, thinking that it must have been one of my nine lives gone, as they say. In due course all bad things come to an end, as do good ones. We returned to Cork harbour where many ships had sought shelter from very similar misfortunes to ours.

When the mail arrived aboard I was notified by my engineer that after Christmas, and my next patrol, I was to leave the *Jessie* and proceed to Chatham barracks. Our Christmas festive dinner proved to be salt pork and biscuits, a real dish I must say! But why worry, in a few days time I shall be home, if my good fairy willed it so. The weather was kinder but I rendered no thanks to the Almighty, because I guessed that with my next breath I would be blaming Him for causing hardships and loss of human life. That seemed like fair comment to me.

The days seemed to fly by and, once in harbour again, I did my packing and, with some mixed feelings, I took leave of my shipmates; like a band of brothers we had endured so much together and, despite all their blasphemy and vile oaths, they were a fine bunch of boys. I even paused to look at *Jessie*, she had got me in and out of such scrapes but I loved her. She had made me swear, cuss, and lose any piety I may have had. So, as I left her, the lads wished me luck and I raised my cap to *Jessie* as I sped away to start new ventures.

Chapter 16 – Promotion and HMS Ceres

In the forenoon of New Year's Day 1918 I arrived at Chatham barracks and, after being told about my quarters, or mess to be nautical, I was given ten whole days leave! I sent a telegram home, had a wash and brush up, packed my bundle, in the usual blue handkerchief used for such purposes, and I went home. Again I arrived to a lovely welcome and all the home comforts. I hardly knew how to express my joy, perhaps I was a little – I think that the word is – bewildered and, of course I was excited. To have ten days leave, ten days of peace, was a Godsend, especially after the previous couple of years of real hardship. Louisa, my wife, bless her, had scraped a little more cash together, to spend. I also had some but not much. We planned how to make the most of it. A theatre or two, a music hall, the cinema or maybe an evening ding-dong on the piano, which was our only merry making in the home in those days. We made the best of it with our home cooking; which, after my recent times seemed very special, and I felt I was living like a king. I made new friends, met our neighbours, and lost my coolness to the ladies. Just as well perhaps, because then I felt a new person with higher ambitions.

After a good rest, and entertainment, I returned to Chatham and I was detailed for an oil-fuel training course of about three weeks. I had to study hard at these methods of oil-fuelled turbines, which were new to me and, at the time, the latest modern methods. These turbines were now coming into general use and I eventually mastered the new technique. After my test, I was listed to appear before the engineer captain and commander for a professional and personal examination for petty officer. I was not nervous about it; in fact I was quite confident. It might sound like it but I do not think I was being big-headed about it; I knew that I had studied all the theory very well and thought, "Now for the interview."

It was quite something to get praise from the higher ranks, after they had read my reports and it gave me a big boost at the start of the examination. Then, one after another, they plied all their questions, some of which were domestic and some, technical. I did not get confused and answered them all in strict rotation, politely excusing myself, as I changed to the next answer. Above all, I did not hurry. They were very pleased with my answers and my demeanour. I never spoke unless there was a question, did not butt in, tried not to miss a single detail, always answered as though I was in charge and they appeared to like all that. At the end of this grilling, the captain asked, "As you are so keen, which ship, or which kind of ship, would you like to sail on? You can have your choice."

"I would like to go on a fast modern light cruiser," I replied, "one with fuel oil." The captain enquired of the other officers which ships were refitting or being built, and as I listened I heard the name *Ceres,* which I knew to be one of the crack cruisers. So, I asked if I could go to her. My request was granted and I was told that I would be made a petty officer in a few months. I had thought that I might be too young but, *no,* they wished me luck and I was drafted to the *HMS Ceres.*

My new ship was lying in dock at Hull and I arrived on board at about 10 p.m. on the 20th February 1918. I reported to the Jonty, which is Navy slang for master at arms. Most of the ship's company was on leave and the ship was untidy because of workmen still being aboard. He said that I had better go on leave too. I could not believe my ears. However, I knew that I had only two shillings in my pocket. He said there were no more trains to London until 4 a.m. and I said I would go straight away, if I could have a free pass. He said, "Go and get ready and by then I'll have your leave pass and railway voucher ready for you." I thought he might change his mind, so I left the ship quickly and, all in darkness, with the help of workmen directing me, I found my way out of the docks and walked to Hull station. At about 1 a.m. I arrived at the station, which seemed deserted, with no lights and no movement. I was wandering around full of expectation of soon being home, when a young lady approached and asked if she could help me. I explained my intention and she said, "Come with me and have some refreshment." I was led to a large blacked out room and inside, what a grand sight to behold. My chaperon suggested I have some hot food. I had to tell her that I needed my little bit of money for my transport at King's Cross in London but, she explained, there was no charge, as the ladies in Hull had volunteered their services and that the townspeople had found the money. She brought bacon, eggs, tea and toast for me. There were dozens of other service lads in the same room, some of whom were asleep in bunks. After eating, she told me the time of the next train was about 5 a.m., suggested I had a couple of hours sleep and that I would be awakened in time. I did as I was told but felt sure I must be dreaming. I was awakened with a tray of hot tea and toast, and a smile. She was so ready to help me that I still think she must have been an angel, in human form. I noticed a box on the counter, I put one of my two shillings in it, I was never more pleased to spend a shilling in my life. I then got on the train and travelled to King's Cross.

 I arrived home about 10 a.m. and met Louisa carrying refreshers for her and Uncle Matt. When she saw me she dropped the lot. I had to explain that I could not have warned her of my arrival. She soon got over seeing a ghost and after an affectionate greeting I was subjected to the, "how, when and where", questions. Recovering my breath and composure, I had to tell her I had come home with only fourpence in my pocket. But she was in a loan club, which we borrowed from and then we settled down for another ten days of peace and quiet. There was no riotous living, as we had to eke out our money.

 I returned to Hull and saw my new sweetheart, SS *Ceres* properly for the first time. She looked great and I felt proud of her already. She was to carry me many thousands of miles, to many adventures. There she was, freshly painted, in light grey, about 400 feet long, 4,000 tons displacement, a hull like a destroyer, with a high forecastle and a low main deck. She had all the latest inventions: a tripod mast with gunnery control tower, five six-inch guns and eight by twenty-one inch torpedo tubes. Her maximum speed would be about 34 knots. She was that deceptive, that from the horizon, she would look like a destroyer.

So, all the hands were to get busy scrubbing, cleaning, and getting her 'Bristol fashion'. After touring the ship I knew I would be comfortable and be able to get a good sleep in my hammock. We had a crew of 400 officers and men. I saw the engineer commander who said he would give me various duties to learn the rudiments of the ship. My first duty was water tender in the foremost boiler room, where two huge boilers were situated. These were fifty to sixty tons each and were oil-fired, so no more coal dust! I would be able to work with clean dry suits on and not soil my hands, and what a change that would be.

To enter the boiler room one passed through an air lock, which was a compartment with two doors. We would open one door, get inside and then shut the outer door, open the second door, step out and close that door. This routine was necessary owing to the air pressure needed to burn oil-fuel. Failure to close the doors would cause a flash back and some ratings got severely burnt when the flaming oil blew back. Air pressure was maintained by huge fans of about seven feet in diameter.

There were gauges indicating the level of water in the boilers and it was my duty to see that there was neither too much nor too little. There were three powerful pumps and I had to be prepared for any change of speed. I also had to keep the steam pressure at 275 pounds per square inch. If it reached 280psi the safety valve would lift, which was classed as an 'offence' and not good watch keeping. So, I had to be prepared at all times and be alert. I wondered how she would behave at sea in bad weather. I did not have long to wait to find out. We were ordered to join the Grand Fleet. The main base of Grand Fleet was at Scapa Flow but we joined our squadron at Rosyth. There were five special service ships in our squadron: our flagship, which was the *Cardiff,* then us *Ceres, Caradoc, Cassandra* and the *Calypso*. We never dropped anchor but passed ship wires through our allotted buoys, ready to slip at a moment's notice. So, we always had to have steam up and be ready to sail.

Our squadron looked imposing in a straight line just east of the Forth Bridge. As for our big brothers; we were near the

Repulse, *Renown*, *Lion* and *Tiger,* which were battle cruisers of around 30,000 tons each. Some of these ships had fifteen-inch guns, firing a shell of nearly a ton, whilst our six-inch guns fired shells of one hundredweight. Opposite us, on the Firth, was a battle squadron consisting of the *Barham*, *Valiant* and *Warspite* and under the Forth Bridge, at Rosyth, lay the *Queen Elizabeth*, or the *Lizzie* as she was called, with Admiral Beatty aboard.

The Fleet was always at readiness and had three routines: 'stand by to skip'; when everybody was at their stations and ready to proceed to sea; 'one-and-a-half hour's notice', which meant the crew could relax in their quarters and then there was 'four hours notice', during which, watches could go ashore and stretch their legs for a few hundred yards. At the 'four hours notice' we could visit Dunfermline or Inverkeithing. There we saw swarms of sweethearts and wives on the grassy slopes, always watching out for their favourite ship and, of course, the leave-boats. They would get to know our habits and were always scenting when a 'flap' was on by the amount of our activity.

Once again I was on the 'active list' and ready for the front line of battle should the enemy show its nose out of harbour. One evening, during darkness, we slipped our moorings and were off to sea at twenty knots, our usual cruising speed. With our other ships, we steamed in single file, keeping the same distance from one another by means of shaded lights over the sterns, which gave just sufficient light to the following ship. On through the night and across the North Sea we sailed, with our big brothers out of sight, but never far behind, and, on each of our flanks, there were nine or ten destroyers. Towards the Bight and Jutland, we went, sweeping along and keeping clear of enemy mine fields and always with extra lookouts. Behind a barrage of mines, in the Heligoland Bight, the Germans exercised their cruisers. Our guns could reach seventeen miles, and as we spotted them, we opened fire and so did they. However, after a salvo or two, they retreated behind a smoke screen. It was my first a taste of sailing at high speed, with the ship throbbing and ploughing through the sea. To watch my squadron, doing the same, was thrilling and filled me with pride. This trip on the *Ceres* convinced me that I was now on a tough ship, and that gave me added confidence and we always knew our big brothers were nearby. These sweeps were a frequent occurrence but our stay at sea could never be long, two or three days, and then we would head back to harbour again to take on oil. It would be of no use meeting the enemy when our fuel was low and, of course, we always had to go across the North Sea to meet them, thus using much of our fuel up. In the end, it was our wits against their wits.

When I was not on watch in the boiler room, my action station was in the forward magazine. I had to be ready to open our flooding valves, if ordered, in the event of fire. I made it my business to get to know every valve, in every part of the ship, because I thought that as well as saving my own life, it might save the lives of others. This survey took me some weeks to carry out. I had charge of the 'forward fire brigade'. I would have to direct operations by phone from the bottom of the ship, so I had to learn the position of all the watertight doors, which were the means of securing various compartments in case they were flooded, or the fire-main fractured. Our phones excluded most noises, except gunfire, but to be heard on them, we had to shout like lunatics. With tiers of live shells near at hand, it was a bit nerve racking and it took a great effort to stay unruffled and composed.

When on duty with others, and sharing the same excitement of imminent danger, it was always necessary to watch each other, for signs of hysteria, which could be very contagious. Self-control was a must. Naval discipline and training instilled that in us.

On occasions 'action stations' would be simulated and officers would shout imaginary damage situations. For me it was a case of using my wits, having to know the whereabouts of all transverse and longitudinal bulkheads and watertight doors. This was in order that I might instruct the fire fighters where supplies of water were to be found, and if flooding was needed, which compartments to isolate. It was all very interesting. But I was always hoping that it would never be wanted in reality. At the end of 'action stations' the bugler would sound the 'secure', and we would revert to normal and resume our chores, and hobbies.

Sailors' hobbies were very varied, with things such as painting pictures, model making, mat making, playing games or even knitting. A mess deck with perhaps a hundred lads would be fascinating and intriguing. For myself I did drawings of the ship, and made mats for home use. I was always loaded with something, when going on leave. To save us looking like beatniks, I even tried cutting hair. As regards mat making, patience in preparing material was highly important. Old socks, jerseys, comforters, winter pants, of which there were always plenty around, would all be washed thoroughly, unravelled, perhaps dyed, dried out and then made it into balls. It kept us from getting morose.

Gambling with cards was carried on, without permission, and Housey-Housey, bingo, was played, with a limit of a ha'penny for the stake. In fine weather we would have a singsong on the upper deck with a banjo or mandolin. We also had a piano in our recreation room and a cinema projector. It was our picture palace, with just one reel silent features. To accompany the films,

Fred's pencil drawing of HMS Ceres

our pianist would play appropriate music such as sad, romantic or exciting. Limited space made it necessary to watch films in shifts called red, white and blue, which gave us all an opportunity.

A young lieutenant started a concert party which evoked a lot of interest and fun, the trouble was that the lads had to send home for ladies' clothing. Can you imagine the fun when we got the supplies from the ladies? Good-looking chaps, young ones, were selected. Funnily enough, I was selected, but not because I was good looking. I was rather coy about this but my word how bigheaded could I get. Having learned our parts, there came that critical time of the dress rehearsal. What with false hair, powder and rouge, the dresses (yes, with undies) and high heel shoes... I will leave it to your imagination! But it was all good clean stuff. Three junior officers joined in and what fun we had with them. I played the part of a girl but, safety in numbers, I thought. Our revue was very good, so we entered it for the squadron 'do', when we were on 'four hours notice' in harbour. The Marine band helped us out and the Navy had fitted out an old hulk, an empty shell of a ship, with a stage, props, and seating to accommodate hundreds. She was towed alongside and invitations were signalled to other ships. The 'theatre goers' arrived by all sorts of boats and were in evening attire, blue suits and, as it was after sunset, without collars. Officers came with their lady friends, who must have blushed at times with our crudeness. But, on the whole, it was a very good show. Imagine the uproar when a sailor would kiss a 'girl' and begin canoodling, and the ribald remarks and laughter about the dresses. We got applause, in full measure and of course there had to be lots of repeat shows, for all the other watches. The fever caught on with other ships' companies and I must say it was a godsend, which relieved the monotony of waiting for the Germans.

Well, that was play and now for work. By day, I was given a new job; I was in charge of a party of lads whose job it was to inspect, clean and paint in confined spaces, such as 'double bottoms', which referred to the space between the hull of the ship and her inner bottom, a distance of two feet. Each rib of the ship had an aperture just big enough to crawl through for perhaps fifteen feet. I had to test the air for foulness or gas with a safety lamp and other equipment. Sometimes it was necessary to pump out the gas, which was mainly carbon dioxide. After reassuring the men, I instructed them to talk, whistle or sing, whilst they worked, in order that I could hear each of them. While I could hear them I was sure of their safety. Then, on my all clear signal, work would start. If one of the men became silent, and it could happen very quickly, I would warn the others and have to go and drag the victim out, which was a dodgy job. For this we received nine pence a day extra in danger money. But if one obeyed the rules it was quite safe. Oil fuel tanks required similar constant surveillance, and a careless moment in them was enough to render a man unconscious or 'under the influence'. Often we had to call for assistance to help rescue those overcome. As I had the trust of the engine officers, I was kept on this odious job. I did not mind, because getting the confidence of my superiors meant such a lot to me. I knew that would have its rewards, and besides, it was extra cash!

Talking of extra cash, I remember, at about this time, there was much unrest in the Grand Fleet. One battleship's crew had refused to go to sea, which caused much consternation among our superior officers. So much so, that a high official from the Admiralty was sent from London to investigate the trouble but no one was arrested for mutiny. When their case was put forward by the lower deck, it transpired that their main grouse was about the comparison of munitions workers' money to their own. The immediate response from the Admiralty was a generous pay rise all around, officers as well. I was very pleased about this, as my own pay was a little over a pound a week, plus about six shillings 'wife allowance'. I forget now the amount of our raise but it was generous indeed, with extra allowances for clothing and victualling, together with other benefits. This meant that the trouble ended and it gave us all fresh hopes.

The whole fleet was ordered to sea and we all proceeded to Scapa Flow to join the Northern Fleet. This armada put to sea in battle array, an impressive sight to see. There were over forty battleships, together with an American squadron of thirty fast, light cruisers and flotillas of destroyers and submarines. We were on a large-scale manoeuvre in the direction of the German coast. Each flagship had an observation balloon with lookouts. I was wondering why we were all out. Was there a big battle imminent? But after two or three days of exercising we returned to our bases.

It seemed that the Fleet had been awaiting the right weather conditions of a moonless night and a calm sea, which eventually arrived. It was April 22nd, the eve of St. George's Day when the Harwich Forces and the Dover Patrol were alerted for a big operation, which had been prepared months beforehand. The Grand Fleet put to sea and proceeded towards Heligoland and Jutland. During the evening the Harwich and Dover forces had started their mission of escorting some very old cruisers, filled with cement, towards Zeebrugge to block that harbour by sinking the old cruisers and preventing U-boats getting out into the Atlantic. The plan was for the Grand Fleet to cut off the German Fleet and engage them in battle, which could have been fatal for the Germans. However, the German fleet remained in port. But the operation at Zeebrugge was a complete success in spite of fierce German resistance and heavy losses on both sides. The U-boats were bottled up in port, and that eased our losses in the Atlantic. The Grand Fleet remained on patrol and out of sight while the Harwich and Dover forces returned to their bases, and as the Germans did not show themselves, eventually the Grand Fleet returned to base, while the US cruisers covered their tracks. St. George's Day was a day to be remembered by the Navy.

It was springtime and the news from France was improving. The Americans were there in large numbers and a big push was expected. The German troop losses were appalling, and had reached well over a million. Our losses had been appalling too and too awful for the authorities to admit. The suffering must have been terrible for our Tommies. Large numbers suffered from shell shock, which was due to the stress of the gunfire. So terrific was the noise that it could be heard in Kent.

My brother George had been sent home, because his nerves were wrecked. He was invalided out after breaking down under the strain of being in the artillery in Flanders. Thousands of others had suffered from poison gas, which killed, blinded or maimed men for life. A sacrifice which, unfortunately, was soon forgotten in peacetime.

Chapter 17 – The Armistice and SS Cassandra

To think of home leave at that time was out of the question. So to give Louisa a change, I arranged a holiday for her. I found lodgings in Dunfermline and obtained special leave for about six hours to meet her at Edinburgh. It was summertime, the weather was kind, and it would give her a break for a month. The digs were very comfortable and need I say how we felt, I think you will understand. Having got her settled in, with a grand old lady with whom she made friends, she soon met other sailors' wives. They were all getting to know the routine of watching from the green slopes of Inverkeithing. Louisa could look out for my squadron and, naturally, my ship. We were always slipping out to sea, after dark, on some stunt or exercise, which usually took about three days. Then as the ships steamed back in to tie up, the girls would wave to us, whilst wearing vivid colours, so that on board we could recognise our particular sweetheart. Louisa was among friends and enjoying a break from the London air. On 'four hours' leave, the most we could do was get together for a chat. I will never forget those times when just the two of us got together for those brief spells. At each parting, neither of us betrayed our innermost feelings but each of us must have been wondering if we would meet again. Then, what a crowd there would be at the jetty, all giving their wives and sweethearts final hugs and kisses, and then off on board until next time. Sunday mornings, when we mustered for church service, was a time when the girls could watch the movements on the ships and hear our hymn singing.

On board when the boilers had to be cleaned from inside we would lay-up for a few days and we could have leave, in watches, which relieved the monotony. Louisa was looking quite bonny, laying in the sun and getting tanned. We were always hoping that our cash would last out and that somehow we could manage for a few weeks.

As I have said previously, the *Ceres* was in a 'Special Service Squadron' and we never knew exactly where we were, or why we were there. It so happened that one morning my squadron put to sea with nine or ten destroyers and steamed due east. All our radios were silenced and we were under sealed orders, which were to be opened at a certain rendezvous. We were doing twenty-five knots, without lights, when darkness closed in on the sea. However, we could see some lights ashore, which could not have been the enemy coast. Shortly we saw lights on the other side of us. Were we following a zigzag course, but where were we? During the night we altered course and steamed south, and still there were lights on the starboard beam. We were guessing where we were, when 'action stations' was sounded and then 'stand by'. Our speed was reduced and meals were served at duty posts, which consisted of bread and bully beef. As dawn broke, our ships got busy sweeping down in the open sea with no land now in sight. Any ship which we sighted, the crew was taken aboard one of our ships and then their ship was sunk by gunfire. The crews we brought back to England. In our sweep we sank nineteen vessels, chiefly trawlers. One, a German armed trawler defied us and fired his small gun at us until his boiler blew up and then still he refused to lower his flag. So, a destroyer sank her at point blank range. The skipper was rescued and brought aboard the *Ceres*. Our captain let him retain his sword and congratulated him on his defiant stand against overwhelming odds.

We were going south again during the middle watch, midnight to 4 a.m., and it was a watch of suspense, with everyone wondering where we were going. Each clang of the bridge telegraph would signal a varying of speed. It was making us edgy and with nobody saying anything, it made us uneasy. Suddenly the silence was broken by our small fleet opening fire and creating a hell of a din. But who were we firing at? There were no returned shots. It later transpired that a secret service agent had been landed by a destroyer's whaler. His purpose was to purchase newspapers the ensuing day. But all the next day we did not know where we were. We cruised the open sea, saw no shipping and then, as darkness fell, we went south at full speed, flashing searchlights and firing our guns for about an hour, after which we returned northwards at high speed.

We were ordered to place explosive charges of TNT between the boilers and engines and warned that should we run aground we were to set timers on the charges and to abandon ship. It was a nerve-racking time, with explosives so near to the boilers. The suspense and wondering what would happen next, made us on edge. On going off watch, I went to watch what was happening from deck. It was still dark and I saw lights ashore, which seemed very close. Then we eased our speed, steaming west, with all the ships in line ahead. That meant we must be homeward bound. We could see a rocky coast, and so close. Our speed reduced further and as dawn broke the land gradually disappeared, until it was hardly visible. Then 'lo and behold' there was the Grand Fleet, which had been cruising about waiting for us.

When the story unfolded, we learned that we had steamed through the Skagerrak and Kattegat to the Baltic and that our mock battles had been an attempt to invite the German Fleet out from the Kiel Canal. Our Grand Fleet had been waiting off Jutland, and the coasts we had seen were Norway, Sweden and Denmark. Our minelayers had mined us in, leaving just a narrow gap for us to return, hence our orders to blow ourselves up, on the event of going aground, and make for the shore and internment. Luckily for us, it was not necessary. All apprehension and strain were now passed and we were in good company as we sailed for Blighty.

All the Neutrals we had captured were repatriated and the Germans interned. On arrival at our moorings I was allowed shore leave and we were asked not to mention our exploit to anybody, even our relatives, but there was quite a stir ashore among the ladies, who already knew where we had been. My wife showed me a newspaper, which told how we had, "Swept the Skagerrak and Kattegat under the Germans' noses."

It was always a lovely sight, as we lay in the Firth, to see our wives and sweethearts waving from the shore. But this was soon to stop. We were told that no more leave would be granted until the war was over and we were advised to send our women folk home. "Now what's cooking?" We wondered.

Our Tommies were at last gaining the upper hand in France and the Germans were feeling the grip of our blockade. It seemed the rot had set in on the German front, their casualties were mounting every day and there was unrest in their navy.

So, it was that I saw Louisa off from Edinburgh as she left for London. She was fit and well, after her well-earned rest and change of scenery. But these partings were such that innermost feelings had to be suppressed. We could only live for the moment. Off she went with a wave, maybe a tear in her eye, and best of all, a smile. All I could think was that eternal hope, that I would be spared and come back. Back on board ship everyone was in a similar frame of mind. Our patrols across the North Sea became more frequent.

At the end of August I received news that I had been promoted to acting petty officer, which meant that I took charge of a boiler room. I felt very confident about that and, let me say, I also felt very proud. I intended to do my utmost to prove myself, whatever may betide me. To control a boiler room was a real technical job, which involved controlling the burning of oil efficiently. My first experience of full speed was somewhat frightening: everything was turned on full and the oil was heated to flash point as it arrived at the thirty-six sprayers, each with a maximum output of 900 pounds an hour. That, together with the high air pressure in the boiler room, made the atmosphere like Dante's Inferno. Another petty officer watched the water level, while the stokers watched for my hand signals, as it was a frightful din and voices were as nothing. By then, I knew where every valve was, even in the dark and, if our lights failed, this knowledge would help me to keep calm. In such a case I was hoping I would keep control of myself and not lose my head. The senior engineer came down below and watched me, to convince himself, once and for all, that I could take charge at sea. He never spoke, but just gave me a smile, a pat on my shoulder and he was off. Whilst on watch I was always thinking of what might happen; there could be a leaky boiler, a fractured pipe or a pump might pack up, which was a horrible thought but we were drilled and drilled for this sort of thing, so that it eventually became normal practice. But in the Navy all the vital auxiliary services were duplicated, which proved very helpful. It was quite a thrill to feel the ship throbbing at thirty knots or more. At full speed even the boiler fronts seem to pulsate, an eerie feeling, and, because of the glare, furnaces could only be viewed through dark blue glasses. Then, when the telegraph clanged 'half-speed', swift adjustments had to be made to prevent safety valves from screaming. Once that was sorted things settled down and our tensions eased. However, suddenly dropping our speed from full to half meant that all the heat from the raging furnaces had to go somewhere and the temperature in the boiler room rose rapidly to 120 or 130 degrees, quite warm, but that was our job.

Meal times in the petty officers' mess were different from the old *Jessie*. We had real cups and saucers and a batman to see to our needs. This all made me feel a little important and that my status had improved, and the extra money was especially welcomed.

About October the whole Fleet at Rosyth was stricken with a flu epidemic. At first the victims were relieved of their duties, and we performed duties in two watches, four hours on and four hours off, while the remainder of the crew were feeling groggy. But then as every ship became affected and insufficient numbers were left on duty for ships to put to sea, the Admirals became worried in case of the need for urgent action. Orders were issued to carry on our routine. We put to sea and went on watch even though our knees were knocking, our heads were splitting and we had aches and pains, and were feeling horrible. Sometimes men were lying down on the boiler room plates, hoping that no spasm would arise. It was a week, or ten days, before this epidemic died down, and not before it got a lot of the 'higher-ups' very worried, because we had not been fit to engage the enemy. However, it passed, Jerry missed his chance to catch us groggy and all was well. We were not allowed to mention the flu epidemic in our letters and they were always censored.

Eventually everything got back to normal. The news from France was very encouraging and our Atlantic convoys were now getting through. About mid-October there especially seemed to be an air of expectancy. News had leaked out that people in Germany were revolting over their food shortages and their heavy casualties on the Western Front. They were cracking under the strain. The news boosted our own morale and at last gave us that long awaited uplifting feeling. Each day brought new rumours, or 'buzzes' as we called them in the Navy. Then on orders from Admiral Beatty each ship in our squadron was given ten days advance leave, men would have to remain on board during the annual refit, with just a few ashore. All long leave in the Navy was stopped until the war was over. A sure hint, we thought, that the armistice was near.

On November 11th 1918 the great moment arrived, an armistice was signed by the German High Command. At 11 a.m. all guns were silenced in France, and we received the news about 11.30 a.m. A signal was made by the flagship, 'splice the main brace', meaning two issues of rum ration and then we had a church parade on all the ships, with ships' bands playing hymns and captains taking the service. One and all were thankful to the Almighty.

Can you imagine our thoughts, whilst standing bareheaded and in profound silence? Thinking of the millions of killed, maimed and driven insane. Casualties, in millions? It was awful, in a civilised world. Or were we in a civilised world?

I had sad news from my dear Louisa that she had received the letter[e], one which she had long dreaded receiving, that her brother Alf had been killed in France in October 1918 just six weeks before the end of the war. He was a machine gunner, killed in the big push at St. Quentin. He was probably blown to pieces with his crew because his body was never found. He died so near to peace, aged 26. That parting two years earlier, when

---

[e]See Appendix iii**Error! Bookmark not defined.**

he had waved me off at Paddington station with his family around him had been our final farewell.

As the church service continued, I was thinking of my Louisa at home, in mourning for her dear brother Alf. Then, as we were dismissed a signal was made that celebrations would start at 7 p.m.

I settled down to write a letter to Louisa saying how sad I was about Alf. While I wrote, the lads were dancing together on the mess deck and hugging each other like happy children. Staid men, once stern and rough, were now dancing and letting their emotions come to the surface. It was indeed a lovely thing to see happen. Apart from my feelings about Alf, I suppose I was in the same mood. So, I finished my letter saying how excited and happy everyone was at the news of the end of the war.

With all the clatter and din, there was no peaceful nap for the watch keepers, who could not sleep. Even starchy officers broke their standards and rejoiced with us. I suppose some of us became exhausted by all the celebrations and some overwhelmed by the moment, which brought tears of joy and tears of sadness unrestrained. Just a human reaction to the end of four years and three months of war.

I had the last dogwatch in the boiler room, 6 to 8 p.m. and remember, at 7 p.m. the fun was to begin. Only having one boiler alight was not thought to be sufficient power for what was to happen, so I was ordered to flash another boiler to 'stand-by', because there was no knowing what the lads would get up to. At the appointed hour the signal was made and the whole fleet opened up their sirens, which were very loud, whooping out messages in Morse. I had to connect the second boiler to supply their needs on deck, dynamos were all running and all the searchlights were switched on. It was a grand spectacle, which I had a quick glimpse of, as I popped up the ladder. Coming off watch, there was no supper needed and I joined in the fun. The Forth Bridge was lit up by searchlights, as were the crowds of people on the shoreline who were waving flags and going crazy. Some lights were focused on the City of Edinburgh across the

Firth. Scores of whalers and cutters rowed around with men in them playing banjos and all sorts of instruments. The ships' bands were blaring out popular songs and star shells added to the glare in the night sky, which people must have been able to see for miles around. Words will never describe that memorable evening. The trains looked and sounded like toys crossing high up on the Forth Bridge and blowing their whistles. White Ensigns were prominent in the white glare, as were flags of our wartime allies. Strings of bunting were hitched up anywhere they could be flown. Naval routine had broken down and the lads were letting their steam off! It was about 10 or 11 p.m. when the bugler sounded 'secure and pipe down'. Perhaps it was just as well because dancing, singing and shouting does tire one out. I will never forget that hectic night or what it was all about. How we wished our wives had been present. "Surely", I thought, "we must get some leave soon." But we would have to wait and see.

Next day we were back to our routine and my squadron was detailed for another special duty. We painted the ship, overhauled everything, refuelled and stood by to be ready at one hour's notice to slip our moorings. We were wondering if anything was wrong. Then we slipped out to sea on the afternoon of the 16th November and at daybreak steamed due east at twenty knots. We fanned out, line abreast, with each of our five light cruisers about a mile apart. In the distance we sighted a ship, challenged her and signals were exchanged. It was the German cruiser the *SMS Königsberg*, a new ship and freshly painted. The *Cardiff* turned about and took the lead, the others of us lined up, two each side at a distance of half a mile and so we steamed at twenty-five knots back to Blighty. The German ship flew a small ensign, whilst we flew larger ones at our mizzens. The *Königsberg* was carrying the German plenipotentiaries over to receive the terms of the armistice. She was a fast vessel, similar to our ship, and so speed could be increased to over thirty knots and we soon arrived at a bay in the Firth of Forth. The German dignitaries were taken to London, whilst we circled the *Königsberg*, which was at anchor, and waited patiently. After the

Germans had agreed to the terms of surrender of their fleet, they returned, from London and boarded the *Königsberg*, which we then escorted to a rendezvous in the North Sea. Another momentous event had been concluded and so we went back to base again.

Our whole fleet was now preparing for the surrender of the German High Seas Fleet. And so it was on November 20th 1918 the Grand Fleet, the Harwich and the Dover patrols put to sea to accept the surrender of the German naval Forces. We had the honour I mean, my squadron had the honour, of locating the Germans and as dawn was approaching we fanned out in single line abreast towards the rendezvous in the North Sea.

The 21st of November was a typical November morning, damp, murky and with poor visibility. But it was a day I will always remember because it was so awe inspiring, and something to fill anybody with pride. As the dawn broke on the eastern horizon there was a great pall of smoke, signals were flashed to the Grand Fleet and 'action stations' was piped. Torpedo tubes were swung outboard and everybody was on the alert in case of treachery, or a last minute 'do-or-die' action by the enemy. We neared the Germans who were steaming single line ahead about 500 yards apart and doing ten knots. *HMS Cardiff* had the honour of leading the column while *Ceres, Caradoc, Cassandra* and *Calypso* steamed along the German line about 1000 yards away. We were able to observe the armistice terms, all guns had to be depressed, torpedo tubes covered and kept fore and aft. The German ships looked filthy with barnacles on their hulls, a tiny German ensign fluttering at the main and such was their condition that ten knots was their top speed. As the gloom lifted our fleet was steaming in immaculate order of two lines, three miles apart, and one on each side of the enemy. Our ships had their fifteen-inch guns at the ready and huge white ensigns fluttering in the breeze. The *Ceres* had a great silk ensign made by officers' wives for this occasion. And so my squadron took up our position about three miles from the German light cruisers. I'll try and illustrate the scene: there were fourteen battleships, seven light cruisers and astern of them were forty-nine destroyers, occupying about ten miles. This was the German Fleet.

On both sides, and three miles away, was the Grand Fleet consisting of eight battle cruisers, thirty-one battleships, twenty-five cruisers and five American battleships. In the rear there were the German destroyers, accompanied by two cruisers and seven flotillas of destroyers.

A sight like this had to be seen to be believed, so grand and perfect was the execution of the plan. Nothing of its like will ever be seen again. I wondered, "What about the feelings of the German seamen in their ignominious defeat? Surely they must have felt dejected and ashamed." This was a stern retribution but as I thought of those four years, now behind me, I could not raise any compassion for the German sailors. I was just hoping that they would do nothing rash, because both sides would have had heavy casualties. We steamed at ten knots towards the Firth of Forth, and at Harwich our forces escorted the German U-boats and other craft. What a day!

On arrival in the Firth of Forth all the German naval personnel, except for a skeleton crew for each ship, were transferred to German transports and sent home. The Grand Fleet then escorted all the German ships to Scapa Flow where the Germans ultimately scuttled their ships but that is not part of my story.

We tied up, at our usual moorings and took on board large quantities of machine guns, rifles, ammunition, food stores, sledges and reindeer harnesses. Then my squadron was given further orders. "What on earth was going on now?" we all wondered. Our dreams of leave were fading fast. We put to sea again accompanied by destroyers and steamed off again. There was no more darkening of the ship routine and it was a treat to be able to see our companions' lights. We arrived at the Skagerrak and Kattegat and anchored off Copenhagen, where we were given some shore leave. The Danes were all smiles and greeted us as good friends in their lovely clean city.

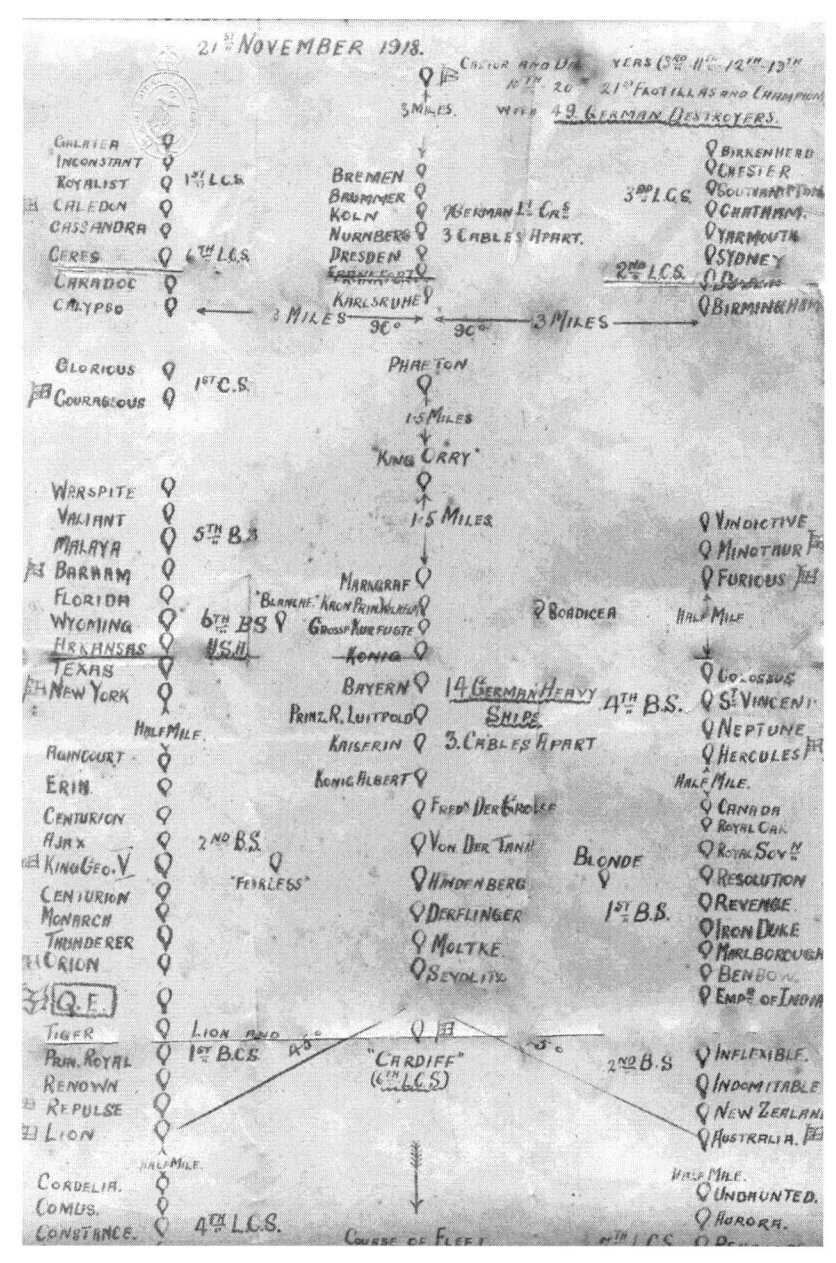

Fred's copy of the plan of the surrender of the German navy November 20th 1918

Hundreds of our ex-prisoners of war, with Danish Red Cross staff, came marching into the docks. We were restrained from chatting with them, but the authorities could not stop us buying cigarettes, matches and sweets and throwing them to our happy and excited Tommies. They were singing, "Take me back to Dear Old Blighty…" The Danes joined in with the Tommies' happiness and made us all very welcome. When the transport was full, she slowly steamed off, homeward bound between the two lines of the ships of our small fleet. Signal flags were hoisted: 'Good luck' and 'Bon voyage', while the *Cardiff's* band played, "Home Sweet Home" and "Rolling home to Merry England". The Tommies got to every vantage point on the transport, in the rigging, up masts, waving frantically. All our sirens were hip-pip-pipping a real send-off as the transport slowly steamed away into the distance, with two minesweepers as escort. I could not help thinking of the hundreds of wonderful reunions to come.

After our few days in Copenhagen we prepared to resume our journey. The weather at that time was terribly cold, with bitter east winds blowing and the temperature was falling fast, making the seawater sluggish with lumps of ice floating about. We steamed eastwards into the Baltic, seeing parts of Sweden and then the open sea. The scene was changing with freezing, bitterly cold easterly winds and gales, which froze the spray on our deck as our bows rose and fell. As evening approached, more ice was seen.

We dropped anchor at Libau[f], a town on the Lithuanian coast held by German troops in charge of a prisoner of war camp. We left next forenoon leaving one cruiser there while the remainder steamed slowly out with a Russian pilot aboard our flagship *Cardiff*. We steamed slowly north with it getting colder and colder, and our superstructure covered with ice. Even our boats were frozen to their davits, and the rails and gun shields were draped with ice, which looked like lace. I suppose it was pretty

---

[f] Liepāja – a town on the Eastern Baltic coast – in *German Libau*.

but I hated it, especially when the temperature fell to 20 degrees below zero. Not a warm feeling!

I was waiting to go off watch in the engine room when at about 11.30 the ship shuddered, the deck plates were lifted and we suddenly listed over as the steering went hard over. There were no signals from the bridge and the boiler room gauges were steady. I wondered if we had struck a mine or something, because the steering engine had returned the helm amidships and the telegraph clanged 'stop engines' followed by 'slow astern'. I knew something was amiss and so, on being relieved, I put my duffel coat on and went on deck. What a spectacle I saw. It seemed the *Cardiff* had swept up a mine with her para vanes and the *Cassandra* was hit amidships just aft of the tripod mast. We had to take evasive action and came to a stop a couple of hundred yards on her beam. With all searchlights focused upon her, the *Cassandra* was down in the bows and she was slowly sinking. All ships were frantically trying to free their lifeboats which were frozen hard to their davits. The ropes, or falls as we call them, about two inches in diameter, were like solid wire, and axes and hammers were used to try to free them. The Carly floats were in a similar condition. We worked in feverish haste, although the *Cassandra* was not sinking fast, but her main deck was at an angle of about 20 degrees.

The state of sea prevented destroyers going alongside the stricken cruiser, whose crew was desperately trying to strengthen her bulkhead to withstand the strain as water reached the main deck forward. Her stern lifted from the sea exposing her propellers, and the captain ordered 'abandon ship', but how? The freezing water would have killed many. However, the Admiral ordered three destroyers to attempt the rescue of the 390 crew. The first destroyer misjudged her distance and failed to lie alongside, the second also failed but the third, with a young lieutenant in charge came out of the darkness, her hailer telling the *Cassandra* crew to, "Stand by to jump!' On he came at high speed, but when he neared the *Cassandra's* stern we thought he would ram her, but no! He put his engines full astern and seemed to glide close alongside. "Jump now, you have a minute!" came the voice over the loud hailer. And they jumped as the destroyer throbbed alongside. Everybody did the right thing and escaped, except for one sailor, who jumping too soon, was crushed between the two ships. The rescue was over in about three minutes. The destroyer drew away amid the cheers from us all. Most of the crew were in night attire of just flannel vests, pants and socks, not a warming thought. The *Cassandra's* captain had been left on board, on his bridge and our captain pleaded with him to leave but he declined. So our boys got a dinghy free and it was lowered to the sea by manpower, a freezing cold job. Then an officer and two seamen were sent with orders to get the captain, whatever, even if they had to arrest him. We prepared to receive some of the rescued sailors. Our small boat had got alongside the *Cassandra,* which was now poised at 30 degrees or more, with her bows under the water and her stern above. Suddenly her tripod mast lurched over and fell through her foremost funnel. The captain came down from the bridge wading waist deep on the main deck and was shouting into various compartments. An officer from our ship and a seaman boarded and grabbed hold of the captain. He struggled but was overpowered and was brought to us. He insisted on staying on deck gazing at the *Cassandra*, a ship he must have loved. Then he sat on a bollard, a lone figure with tears rolling down his cheeks, as the *Cassandra's* stern lifted higher, until she appeared to be standing on end. Her heavy machinery broke loose and crashed forward with a terrific din and she appeared to hang in the air, poised for her last plunge. There was a ghostly silence and she slid to the sea bottom. The lone captain stood to attention, saluted and then broke down. "What a pity," I thought, "especially now that hostilities had ceased."

After roll call it was ascertained that ten men were missing or killed. Killed outright, we hoped. One hour after the *Cassandra* was struck, a short service was held and then we were on our way north again. The *Cassandra's* crew was sent to Copenhagen to embark on a transport for home. The *Ceres* with a destroyer was detailed to go up the Daugava River to Riga. The river was frozen over but we crashed our way through, a new experience for me, and what a noise that crashing ice made. I adopted wearing two of everything, even two jerseys, as it was 30 degrees below. The only way to distinguish the river from the land was that the river was flat. The ice was so thick that it was safe enough to walk on. In fact, every winter, the Russians lay a tram track on the ice. Once alongside the docks at Riga we took stock. The Russians were in the throes of a bloody revolution against the Tsarist regime and the town was occupied by thousands of German troops who got their marching orders from the Russians as and when transports arrived up the river. The river had to be kept navigable by Icebreakers.

Some of the crew of Ceres at Riga

We were joined by the Canadian Pacific liner the *Princess Margaret* or *PM*, as we called her. Her purpose was to rescue from Russia any British personnel and refugees fleeing the Revolution. There was no activity at all in the docks and little could be seen of any Russians, only the hated German Uhlan Guards. Pilfering of flour and other foods seemed to be very frequent, and some of those caught, children as well, were shot on the spot. Together with the aid of an interpreter, the Estonian men who could handle a weapon were drilled by our seamen petty offices, and were taught how to handle British arms. They progressed quite well and, when they were proficient, they were accommodated in a deserted barracks at the rear of the town. Stocks of war materials were also handed over to them. Our Marines took over sentry duty at the docks and confined the Germans to their quarters. The pilferers earned their ersatz[g] food, which they were stealing, because in order not to be seen they had to tunnel beneath three feet of snow. Their trenches were scratched with their bare hands. The women's clothing was deplorable, much of it made from old sacks, which they wrapped around their legs and feet. They had no boots and wore the dirty skins of animals on their bodies. How they stood the low temperature, I will never know. The food situation was terrible, even for us it was mostly from ration tins. The crew of the *Princess Margaret* made what bread they could for us but we were all rationed.

---

[g] Ersatz – *German* substitute goods or foods.

Chapter 18 – To Riga and the rescue of Mrs Hill

When Sunday arrived, we heard a church bell ringing just like at home, and half the ship's company, bearing the white ensign at their head, were marched to the church. This little church with its steeple seemed to take me back because it was so typically English. Inside members of the, mainly British, congregation crowded around to kiss our flag. They were told that the *Princess Margaret* would take them to England. Some of their men folk had been shot or imprisoned but being told their personal sufferings were at an end, as they were now under British protection, they became calmer and began to smile. Some had walked for miles, through the extreme cold, following the British ships. Their clothing and boots were the worse for wear. How pleased they were to know that we would be taking them back to Blighty. The organist in the church played, "Now thank we all our God," and everyone sang it from their heart, not reverently but with hilarious joy. It was a moment that made me feel good inside. With the white ensign on the altar, the English vicar conducted a service, probably to be his last in that town, before he too left for home. He said that he would still keep the church open, day and night, for any others who sought sanctuary from the Bolsheviks, as the rebel Russians were called.

After the service, we marched back to the *Princess Margaret* with our British refugees in the centre of the column. We had no band so it was, 'March at ease' to war songs like, "There's a long long trail" and "Pack up your troubles in your old kitbag". It made a change for us to have a feminine accompaniment to our singing. The refugees were billeted aboard the *Princess Margaret,* and as we left to rejoin the *Ceres* they cheered us wildly.

The town seemed deserted, and one reason was the huge mass of snow in the streets packed by the roadside. Russian women were chipping the ice from the tram tracks to keep them clear. A narrow footway each side of the street was kept clear, interspersed with breaks so people could cross the road.

To keep warm the sailors played football and violent games of snowballing, but the latter had to be stopped because the warmth of the lads' hands melted the freezing snow into ice and sailors were cut about the face.

As darkness fell so did the temperature fall, down to 30 degrees below zero, and sometimes even colder. A sharp lookout had to be kept on each other's ears and noses, if they turned white there had to be a brisk massage with handfuls of snow to restart the circulation. The massage was very effective and usually brought the red colour back, but if the skin was turning black gangrene was setting in, and perhaps amputation would be needed. So, we observed these golden rules about frostbite. Fortunately, below decks, it was a lot warmer, and one could sleep whilst nice and warm. If nature called during the night, then plenty of clothing was needed as the toilets were on the upper deck. If a strong east wind was blowing one did not linger too long.

British stragglers were still arriving to get passage back to England, some of whom had to be assisted. A destroyer brought us mail, other essentials, and took back our mail to Copenhagen. An icebreaker was needed to help keep a channel navigable for supply ships and us, but the sea always froze again soon after the icebreaker left.

One morning, following a blizzard a few days previously and fresh falls of snow, I was ashore with two others just exercising our legs, when I came across a black bundle of clothes, partly covered with snow. I gave it a gentle kick with my sea-boot and was surprised to discover that it was a human being. I called my mates and lifted an elderly lady out of the snow. Her heart was still beating but only weakly. We started massaging her legs and arms and I held her head with my hands and breathed on her face, holding her close under my duffel coat. We decided to carry her to the *Princess Margaret*, whilst still massaging her and holding her close to our bodies. To our relief, she showed signs of life and began breathing normally. We had found her just in time. The third member of my group rushed ahead to prepare the way and organise hot drinks and blankets and, above all, a cabin. We had 600 yards to go when we heard a weak voice say, "Who are you?"

"We're English," I answered in surprise.

"Thank God!" she replied, and then remained silent. Arriving on board the *Princess Margaret* the steward said, "There aren't any cabins!"

"Are there any German girls in cabins?" Asked my mate, "If so, you can dump them out, because this lady is English." Right away a German countess was ousted out of her single cabin and our lame duck was installed. Hot tea was ready and the cook rustled up some rice pudding. Oh, and a drop of Nelson's Blood, rum! When she revived, with our Doctor's help, she said she was Mrs Hill and wanted my name. I just said, "Call me Smudge, everybody else does." She was comfortable and warm and we left her in good care. I visited her daily with anything dainty I could get from our canteen, such as scented soap, toothpaste, sweets and some English newspapers, which we had received with the last mail. She was very grateful and, considering she was over sixty, had done well to survive. She had been forced to leave her home and estate further up the coast, and her sons had become victims of the Russian Revolution. She was brightening up and feeling a lot better and asked me for my home address and promised to get in touch as soon as she arrived in England. She said that, maybe she might return to Riga to claim her estate, and if so, that I would be rewarded.

Because of transport difficulties our food rations did not seem to improve. Now the war had ended, and it was peacetime, we hoped this state of affairs would soon end. My letters were telling me of the exciting things that happened after the Armistice, which, with my normal luck and to my disappointment, I had missed.

As the days rolled by the weather became atrocious, with the wind biting into one's being. We had to avoid touching any metal on upper decks with our bare hands lest we 'burnt' ourselves.

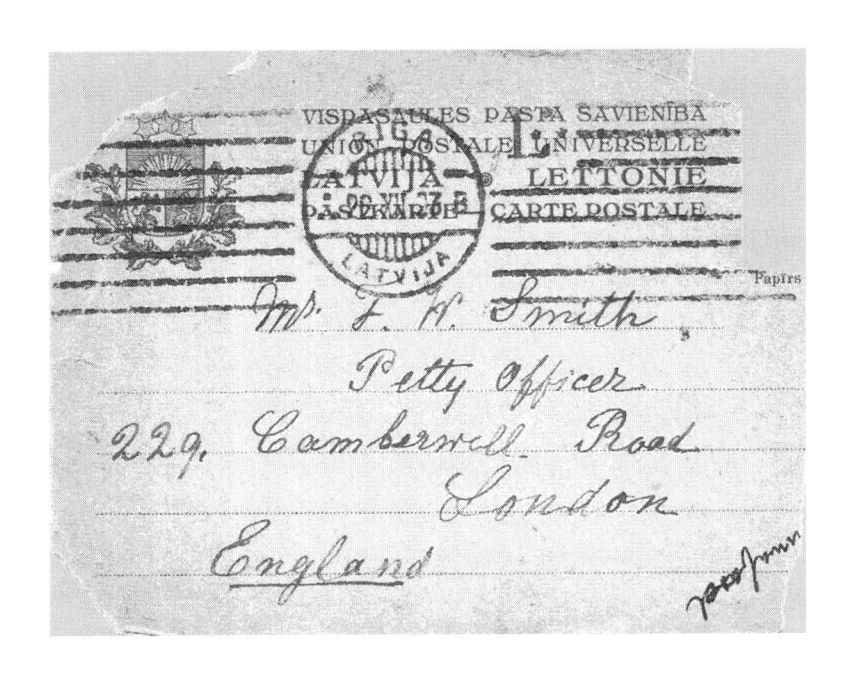

Post card to Fred from the rescued Mrs Hill. After the war she returned to Riga and sent Fred a present.

Riga presented an eerie silence, with hardly any activity, only the drilling and instructions given to the Latvian troops who were not over enthusiastic with what they were doing. The Germans were very sullen and suffering from the cold and rationed food, much of which continued to be pilfered. Women, when caught, would say that they were pregnant and point to their tummies; yet the truth was that bags of flour had been tied around their waists. Our sentries would shut their eyes to most of it but the Germans would threaten to shoot the women. Even if our lads did act without authority this Prussian brutality was halted.

It was found that even to go on watch in the boiler room was not exactly a warm job. One had to put on a jersey and a duffel coat with its hood up. The forced draught was supplied by the fans, the speed of which we kept to a minimum –just sufficient to burn the oil efficiently, and for our own safety, because the air was forced down over our heads and any condensation on the fan casings would freeze and eventually icicles would be seen hanging down like lace. The gauges had a mirror fixed to them, so we could see them, whilst huddling against the side of the boilers. I suppose that sounds fantastic, but there it was.

The temperature of air on the upper decks would be 30 degrees or more below zero and we even had to watch our stock of potatoes carefully, in case they froze. On Christmas Eve a concert and dance, for officers only, took place in the stateroom of the *Princess Margaret*. They invited women of various nationalities, including German, and all were having a rare old party, with food, drinks and other revelry. We tried in our recreation room also to create a little merriment, but with only bully beef and biscuits we could not get in the mood at all. The crew were getting very disgruntled at the way the officers' mess appeared to be getting food from somewhere. The Red Flag was played by some musicians which the lads sang loud enough to be heard by the officers at their party aboard the *Princess Margaret*. Abruptly, their fun and games stopped and they demanded an explanation from us, but as always with such demands, no one volunteered, and everybody kept silent to avoid being arrested as ringleaders. One officer came forward discarding his authority by removing his jacket and cap and appealed sincerely for someone to state their grievance. He promised there would be no incrimination, and so one seaman stepped forward and, hidden from view by onlookers, pointed out our complaints. Well, the outcome was we had a load of meat from shore. When given to the messes it looked awful as it lay in the dish. It was a ghastly greenish brown and yellow looking and no one would touch it. Then a few of us decided to cook a piece by steaming it and it did look a lot different, like leg of beef with gelatine running through it but the taste was delicious. It transpired that we had been given venison. Most were averse to eating it, but thought that as they could eat as much as they liked, more than their ration, it was worth a try. In the end they all enjoyed it and the lads were pacified. Later a destroyer arrived from our flagship *Cardiff*, with further supplies of food and an officer who was to investigate our complaints, return by destroyer and report to our Admiral.

Events ashore were changing, the Leftist troops had mutinied, and an ultimatum had been sent to their barracks giving them to 7.00 a.m. to surrender their arms. Signals were flashed to and fro until finally our five six inch guns were trained on the barracks and at 7.00 a.m. exactly, we fired a salvo which sounded like an earthquake in the cold silent morning air. After three or four more salvos a white flag fluttered over the barracks, they surrendered and were disarmed. After consultations with our higher command we got the news from London to withdraw, as our mission had failed to stem the Russians from revolting. It was a gamble that had not succeeded. "Perhaps," we thought, "now we will soon get our victory leave... and have better food." I told Mrs Hill the news and she was pleased that she would soon be going to see her relatives in Scotland.

Well now, we had to get out of Riga. Although, not too thick the Gulf was frozen over with ice. So, icebreakers worked continuously to free us, but it was slow progress. Once under way our engines were a powerful help; as the ice piled up on our bows we would go astern a little and then charge ahead, and so on through the ice. The *Princess Margaret* followed in our wake as we left Riga and steamed into the Baltic, our course set for Copenhagen. Once there, we spent a couple of days sightseeing among the friendly people. The city was beautiful and clean, with good food of a wide variety. The *Princess Margaret* was escorted by destroyers to Leith, in Scotland, where the refugees were taken care of, while my squadron was dispersed to various dockyards for refits and finally to give us our peace-leave.

The *Ceres* came home to Chatham, the dockyard engineers took over and we all went on a combined leave for three or four weeks, if I remember rightly[h].

Need I say how pleased I was to get home again? I had brought all my kit home with me, including my hammock, all of which I could give a real good clean up, and did it need it. I was able to fix the date of my home coming while at Copenhagen, so my brother and sister, with their family as well, were all waiting to welcome me. It was quite a crowd and what a treat, something I thought I would never enjoy. Partings had not been nice at all, with all the forebodings and uncertainties but our reunions were more than compensatory. I knew that on my return to *Ceres* in late February 1919 she was sailing for a commission in the Mediterranean Sea for two years but I did not tell anyone. I thought, why upset the happiness that encircled me? Well I never! I was invited to lots of parties and, having lost my shyness, seemed to be popular and could enter into all the fun. Of course, it was all homemade entertainment at that time, not like today, when everything is laid on. We had an old piano, which seemed to liven up the evenings, a few drinks and my wife's tasties. Food was still a problem, because there were severe shortages of some items. Worst of all, was the plight of demobilised service men who were still unable to find jobs. The Labour Exchanges had long queues of men seeking work. However, the relief from the strain of the war was a comfortable thought.

---

[h] 14 Jan 1919 -proceeded to Chatham- Went alongside *Calypso* -Service Ratings- going on leave –paid Ratings –proceeded on 38 days leave -3 Sto. P.Os and 2 Lead Stokers joined ship –Leave to watch. : *From Ceres Log.*

I am afraid that I just, 'lived for today'. I was alright and on full pay. I knew I would have to face up to the way of civilian life again soon but I was hoping living conditions would improve by then.

Louisa and I visited theatres and cinemas, sometimes with friends, but we often were quite happy with each other's company, exchanging news and hopes for the future. I did not dare spoil the happiness and tell her I was going away for two years. I did not know a wife could lavish so much loving kindness, Louisa's unselfishness and kindness to others seemed not quite real. But there it was, she was a grand mate to be proud of. Having such a long leave gave me time to assess her real value to me, although I knew we would have to face up to more stern times ahead, but we took things as they came, and each day we became even fonder of each other, if that was possible.

Chapter 19 – HMS Ceres to the Mediterranean

My memory for exact dates of events nearly fifty years ago is a bit vague, but it was late February 1919[i] when I returned to the *Ceres*, my other sweetheart. I told them all at home I would be away for six months, a white lie on my part. Anyhow, my kit was all cleaned up and I had the addition of a foreign service kit of white deck suits and collars. We left Chatham, steamed around the Goodwin Sands and then along the Channel coast, which, now all the lights were on, looked enchanting. Brighton would be our last glimpse of England for a good while. We made for the Ushant light, on the French coast, and steamed down through the Bay of Biscay. Where we ran into a sou'westerly, the Atlantic was in turmoil again. *Ceres* dipped and rolled as the seas rushed over the upper decks but being a cruiser we could still move about below decks.

Our squadron companions *Cardiff*, *Carodac* and *Calypso* were close by and made a wonderful sight. They seemed to be revelling in scooping up the sea and throwing it over their decks, naturally we were doing the same. The waves were thirty feet from crest to the trough, which was forbidding looking but I was now used to it thanks to my previous experiences. We were making a straight course, and it would only be for a day or two, so why worry? Of course, I did not know it, but this was to be my last Atlantic storm.

Having crossed the Bay, suffering some minor damage to upper decks and lifeboats, we sighted Cape Finnistere, in north-west Spain. Then we hugged the coast of Spain and Portugal. The weather remained bad, until we eventually sighted the African and Spanish coasts and veered eastwards. We would soon be in the sunshine. With the two continents on either beam we steamed past Gibraltar into the Mediterranean having travelled about 1200 miles in three days.

---

[i] *Ceres* left Chatham 25 February : *Ceres Log* www.naval-history.net

One afternoon, the ship stopped and with the boom swung out from the side, the lifeboat was lowered and all the non-swimmers were ordered to go overboard. This seemed funny to me. The sea would be about 500 to 600 feet deep, but that was the order. I was surprised at the number of non-swimmers we had on board. Some jumped in near the lifeboat, some from the bridge. Some came to the surface struggling with arms flailing and yelling for life belts, or a boat. So long as they had jumped into the sea, and had got wet all over, their names were ticked off the list. I was spared this caper but only just. For some it was great fun but for others, rather frightening. We did about half an hour of this and then got under way again. The weather was still improving, which did not seem to fit with my normal pattern of luck, but it was true.

In due course we sighted Malta, the sun burnt island which was the Navy's main base in the Mediterranean. What a wonderful panorama we saw as we steamed into the Grand Harbour, with its cream coloured buildings, blue water and silvery beaches all around. Added to this was the sound of church bells, ringing incessantly and all the music from the cafés. Altogether it had a very gay atmosphere. Having tied up at the quay, we took in supplies, re-fuelled, and then half the ship's company were given twenty-four hours leave ashore. The other half would go when they returned. Bob Gillies, one of my mess-mates, was, like me, a tea-totaller. Incidentally, he was also a good boxer. We decided to be buddies on shore leave and avoid the many drunken orgies and fights. We had to use the Maltese boats, which were like gondolas but called Dhaisos. On these the Maltese pushed their two oars, rather than pulling them. The fare was only tuppence. This system of ferrying was a means of livelihood to the Maltese, who were very poor. They were also professional cadgers and very cunning with it. So, care was always necessary when buying anything. To go ashore in 'nobs', or 'duck suits' with blue collars attached, was lovely but the warmth meant you had plenty of dhobeying, washing to the landlubbers, but it did dry very quickly, so it was no trouble.

We landed at Valetta to be greeted by the Maltese, all pestering us and shouting at once, but it was only our money they wanted. After refreshment in a café, we decided to visit the catacombs at Citta Vechia, which the sailors called Shivery Wick. We strolled through Floriana[j] seeing oranges and lemons growing for the first time. Meanwhile cab drivers would worry us to have a ride in their Carozzine, what we called a Garry, which was a horse-drawn landau with sunshade. They were not too lavish – neither were the horses. After being pestered and worried we decided to have a ride. There was not a stipulated fare, and they would say, "What you like, Jose?" And a little bargaining would take place, but it never cost more than a few coppers. Having arrived at the Catacombs we had a guide with a candle to show us underground in the tunnels, which were constructed by the Phoenicians long ago. One had to adopt a stooping position, so low and narrow were the tunnels. Our guide would relate the history, by showing us the millstones and small sleeping niches hewn out of the limestone, which were all very primitive.

We had already paid our guide, but when some good distance underground the candle went out and we were left in darkness. We called our guide but there was no response. Now what should we do in this maze? We waited until we saw the light of another party approaching and heard a voice saying, "I help you, yes?" And so a new guide finished the tour and we paid him. What a neat trick we thought and laughed it off. Reaching the outside we went to the cathedral.

Everything is Roman Catholic on the island. Like so many cathedrals and churches that I have visited, the interiors seemed extravagantly filled with priceless equipment and structures made of various marbles, alabaster and even gold and silver, and all worth a fortune. Yet just outside it was grim and one would see hovels, stricken homes and poverty. The contrast will always haunt me. I wonder what our Lord would say if he were among us today? Would he condone this sort of thing? I am not sure.

---

[j] Floriana (known as 'Il-Furjana') is a town in the Grand Harbour area of Malta, just outside the capital city Valletta.

Maybe there is a reason, but I cannot think of one. Perhaps I am now an agnostic or maybe I am still a mixed up kid.

Fred on the right in his 'whites' with some of his crew mates. The paper is the Daily News

We returned to Valetta and strolled around the high spots of what was like Bedlam-let-loose with every other shop a pub. What I noticed most of all, was that Maltese women wore a peculiar dress, somewhat like a nun, the headdress of which could be swivelled round to hide their faces. It was called the Hood of Shame. When the French army captured the island, all but one of the women had been raped by the soldiers, and that one committed suicide by jumping off a cliff at Valetta. There was a plaque marking the spot. Since then, all women have worn this quaint dress. It appears the custom is now gradually dying out but I saw quite a lot of these hoods. Moreover, it was the custom for women to be chaperoned by a male member of their family when out of doors. Malta was a garrison island at the time of the Holy Crusades and was the origin of the Knights of St John, whose insignia was the Maltese Cross. This was an emblem worn by the Knights when in Palestine fighting the Saracens. Many of the medieval fortresses are still to be seen, and one, in the entrance to Grand Harbour, has towers with an eye, an ear and a nose on them to see, hear and smell an enemy approaching. The harbour was large, almost landlocked, could accommodate the whole Mediterranean Fleet, and was always bustling with activity and music. Children would visit the ships and if a small silver coin was dropped over one side the boys would dive from the other side and get the coin by swimming under the ship's bottom. The sea was very clear and the weather was perfect, with sunshine and warmth all day. Sailors referred to Malta as, "an island of bells, gels, yells and smells", which was a very apt description. Every morning goats, with bells tinkling around their necks, were driven through the narrow streets into the town and the womenfolk would milk them straight into customer's jugs, while the men took the money. We did not use any of the island's milk as they had no cows, at least, I did not see any. We would have tinned milk.

Maltese boys were allowed on board after each meal and they would collect leftovers in pails then wash our plates, knives and forks. The leftovers, which they called 'gashums', were taken ashore to be sold cheaply to the poorer people, of which there were many! The island had very few industries, but the women would still make the famous Maltese lace, once a thriving occupation for the ladies, while the men would work the Dhairos and cabs and carry out any manual work. Large numbers of men worked in the dockyard and their Pidgin English was funny to me after hearing only ordinary English. I was certainly following my intention of seeing the lives of people at the places I visited, rather than booze my time away in pubs, which I am sure many did.

To be on picket duty in the quarter where a colony of prostitutes lived, was to see stark life as it was lived. It was a rendezvous for men to drink and indulge in debauchery. If there was any trouble, I mean serious trouble, involving the service men, a picket's duty was to break it up and arrest the culprit for their own safety. If they had been sober, they would have thought twice about the hovels they went to, and those crucifixes over the beds. What morals some live by, where religion and vice are combined, and it seemed that the church condoned this way for a woman to live. I was able to see at first hand this kind of civilisation, if indeed, that was what it was.

Religious processions seemed frequent, and Corpus Christi was one to remember. The church dignitaries would tour the main thoroughfare, with young girls, dressed in white, strewing flower petals on the roads in front of the fiesta. Then the procession would arrive with a gorgeous canopy held over the cardinal. He was dressed in ceremonial robes, and held the Holy Cross, whilst staring at a relic, which, it was claimed, was a piece of bone from one of their saints. Everyone chanted in Latin, and the populace knelt as the cardinal, with a large number of priests and followers, all playing with their rosaries, slowly passed by. I was interested and removed my cap but I caused a disturbance. It was so easy to offend. And what was my opinion, you may ask? I had little to say. But now when I pray, I pray on my own, as our Lord did, and I say, away with this display of wealth in front of poor wretches who have to subscribe to this sort of thing.

Chapter 20 – Yugoslavia

Ah well, we got our sailing orders. My squadron, slipped their moorings, proceeded in a lovely calm blue sea northeast and passed the foot of Italy. We steamed along the Dalmatian coast and into the Adriatic. A coast of rugged mountains and valleys, which looked wonderful in the clear air and seemed untouched by civilisation.

We proceeded singly, each to our appointed ports, weaving between beautiful islands and finally tied up at the medieval port of Split[k] or Spalato. It had an odour that rather disillusioned one, which was accentuated by the sun's heat, but one eventually gets used to smells. The Yugoslavs were a quaint people, many dressed like brigands, which in fact many were, living in the hills and way-laying people, which meant we travelled in company. There were lots of orphaned hungry children running around in filthy rags. Their parents had been killed by the Germans, often by hanging. The town was demoralised, and no one appeared to know what to do. The urgent need was for relief work and we quickly got into action. Every morning many women would bring lots of flowers to us, mostly roses, a lovely gesture I thought, as they knew we were their friends already. So, first things first; food was arranged, and sheds were built by the Americans and our boys, and straw was used for bedding. They needed to have a good bath and so barrels were sawn in half, a hose was laid on from the ship and then the fun would start: boys and girls were put into the tubs, and much to their surprise they had nearly white skin and could not help looking at each other in wonderment. Cloth was produced and women made garments for them. All the kids wanted to bath every day. Anyway, it was nice to see them smile again.

Among them were two little girls about nine or ten who could speak several languages. They had the freedom of our ship and would go ashore with parties on shopping expeditions. I was in

---

[k] *Split* is now in *Croatia*.

one party of six and we decided to do the girls proud. We had frocks made for them in a pale blue native pattern, with new shoes, and ribbons for their hair. They looked beautiful and they were overjoyed at leaving their rags behind. They became our pets and helped by telling the other children what to do, in their own language. They developed a passion for scented soap and chocolate, how feminine! Anyway it was nice to know we did something worthwhile.

We were always welcomed, with real sincerity, by the town's people. They paraded along the quay every night with torches and would give us a show of Albanian dancing and singing. These simple folk's lives had been made such a misery, and for what? Why, oh why?

Exchanging money was our first problem. We had Kronas and Fillers, which went a long way, and meant that we were able to give the children treats. This was so strange to them because it was the first time they had ever received any treats.

Some resistance soldiers, who had been hiding in the mountains, had returned to the town, and we agreed to teach them the game of football. An afternoon was arranged and a rough pitch chosen. Using primitive tools the pitch was prepared by boys, girls and lots of the town's folk by removing boulders and levelling the ground. Our carpenters made posts from young trees; it was a real do-it-yourself effort. I may mention that it was hot work, in that blazing sun, "but", we thought, "so much better than that ice!" The conversation which we needed to teach them how to play football was made possible by our learned children. This was helped along by lots of gesticulation, which was a common way that foreigners had of making us understand. The Yugoslavs were very hardy, of good physique and speedy runners. We provided lines of bunting and flags to create a little gaiety and pleasure now that the Germans had left. The afternoon of the football match arrived and everyone was wild with excitement. Out came dresses, which had been hidden from the Germans, and it was very colourful.

The Football Match Yugoslavia

Hundreds of the townsfolk were watching and everyone enjoyed every minute of it. Afterwards we were taken back to town and made an enormous fuss of. We were given wine and a little food, which was not very palatable, but of course we did not complain. Then, with more flowers for us, back on board we returned for duty. Some of us decided that, for twenty-four hours, we would work on two watches, four hours on and four hours off and then we would go ashore for the next day.

    A store ship arrived with musical instruments bought by the ship's crew, and so a brass band was formed and we were supplied with a Maltese bandmaster who felt highly honoured. Some of the lads learned a few marches very quickly and when practising on the quay would attract crowds of on-lookers. It was a terrible noise at first, but we suffered it and they improved a lot in a very short while. But they were still not like a military band, oh no!

    One morning, a destroyer arrived and brought mail and newspapers from home. The papers were a week old but no matter. When naval ships came alongside I would always look to see if you knew any of the crew. I recognised a bearded chief stoker, who also recognised me and I invited him aboard for a tot of rum. He was my old Chiefy from *HMS Kale,* the one who had cured me of my seasickness. He looked at me in my petty officer's dungarees and said, "Well done, my lad, you've done well, for yourself!"

"Thanks to you, Chief." I said. After we had had a chat he returned to his ship, and was soon off around the Adriatic on his postman's mission. It was a brief encounter but a warming one. What more can I say; he had been like a father to me. I went on the upper deck to put my letters into sequence before reading them.

Everyone was behaving like quiet little boys reading about their homes, wives, sweethearts and children, and looking at snaps of their relatives and loved ones. We were all in a world of our own with our thoughts of those at home. Because of the aftermath of the War, conditions at home, England, were very tough. Thousands of returned troops and munitions workers were just existing on the dole. That was when war could be so terrible to the victor as well as the vanquished. So foolish, one would think, yet will we ever learn?

Louisa never complained. Like me, she had endured a very rough start to life and so it seemed our lot was to go on suffering. She was always cheerful in her letters, saying how much luckier than many she was. I was in a world of my own with her letters, which I read again and again. Everyone began hastily writing their own letters in order to catch the destroyer returning to Malta. Overland mails were not available then, especially from where we were and so our link, though slow, was established and something to look forward to.

After a few weeks at Split we were set to leave, and turned over our young guides and interpreters to an American cruiser. We had another lovely cruise to Zara, a smaller port than Split but very interesting and medieval. It had plenty of fruit, which was always available and Italian food with lots of garlic and olive oil, not very nice, to us anyway. We were welcomed, and had some youngsters as guides left by the ship which we had relieved, the *Cardiff.* We found the Split money was no good here, and so had to mark our money with its place of origin. The value of money ashore changed almost daily, such was the problem of inflation. We were always working out our sums like children. To us, this money business was perplexing, but our boy and girl guides were worth their keep. In fact, we were in pocket, since they bargained on our side with the shopkeepers. My young interpreter once asked a shopkeeper to exchange, what was the equivalent of an English penny of my money, for 40 coins. The young lad knew that we did not bother with the small coins and would give them to him at the end of the day. He told us he was getting rich!

It was in Zara where we saw the grim side of things; the gallows where men and women had been hanged by the Germans. Women in these parts were real Trojans, tramping for miles over rough terrain, whilst carrying heavy loads on their heads, along unmade roads and tracks, and over rough boulders and rocks. Furniture, such as it was, was also carried on their heads, and sometimes the women had a baby strapped to their backs as well. There were mules and donkeys, but these people could not afford to pay for them.

Men often appeared lazy and were not exactly trustworthy. But they had been used to living by their wits, honestly or otherwise. The whole panorama was one of poverty and sickness amid nature's glorious beauty. There were lovely sunsets among the mountains and islands. Grapes grew in profusion and there were groves full of oranges, which later, when ripe, we relished.

After a stay in Zara we steamed north and arrived at Fiume[1], which was a rather big city, which was also in wonderful surrounding countryside, with a background of mountains, with slopes giving off some lovely colours of various greens. It was beautiful and the temperature was rising, now over 80 degrees, so we had to wear our whites.

We tied up in the docks and added to the quota of warships. There were three battleships and six destroyers, which were units

---

[1] Fiume, now Rijeka in Croatia. *Ceres* arrived there on 19 April 1919 From *Ceres* Captain's log : *www.naval-history.net*

of the Italian navy, a unit of the American navy, a large French cruiser together with British destroyers and submarines, and one of our battleships, the *Ajax* lay anchored just outside the port. The population seemed to be all Italians who would wander through the docks, parading at will in the evening coolness. They were not pleased to see us and in fact resented us. Why this was, we were to learn later. The city had been divided into two, separated by a small but beautiful river. The Yugoslavs were in a section called Susak and were jubilant on our arrival. The Yugoslav girls and women brought us lots of flowers, roses principally, and various fruits. The Italians, it seemed, hated the Yugoslavs, so the latter were glad of our company and showed it by torch light processions, with mandolins and guitars providing music, and making it all very interesting.

The police patrols were composed of English, French, Cingalese[m], American and Italian sailors and soldiers. There was one of each nationality in every patrol, making communication very awkward and at times embarrassing, as the parties patrolled the streets to keep order.

When going ashore, I was struck by the amount of Italian propaganda everywhere. To get a nicer atmosphere I went to Susak. Here the place was orderly, poor perhaps, but the people, in spite of their shortages, were full of kindness. We could change English money to Yugoslav here, which was Kroners and Fillers. It was mainly paper money and the coins appeared to be made of iron. The rate of exchange varied daily, an average of 2,000 Kroners to an English pound, and one Kroner was worth 100 Fillers. So we would have heaps of bits of paper. We always managed to find someone to be an interpreter who we would have to trust implicitly. The children were the most honest, so we would have trailers of youngsters. I suppose they knew that at the end of the day any small change would be left with them.

In the warm evenings the outlying villages were very picturesque, with quaint dwellings and villagers in national

---

[m] Cingalese: Native of Ceylon, now Sri Lanka.

costumes who we watched dancing to their own music. The colours on the mountainside varied every minute in the sunset, and, as we wined and dined with them, it all felt very homely. It was a magical moment with these simple folk, which I shall always remember. It was here we found two lads of about twelve, who knew four languages, so we arranged for them to come aboard the ship, and to chaperone us through any difficulties in town. Their services were simply paid for. From them we learned that 10,000 Italian men and women had been brought to Fiume to colonise the place under the Italian flag and, contrary to the Peace Declaration by the Allies, the Yugoslavs were subjugated under their rule. This was in defiance of the Allied forces terms. The perpetrator of this venture was an Italian patriot named Gabriel D'Ammunzio[n], an airman, poet and very dictatorial charmster, whose propaganda to the populace was very forceful. He was bitterly disliked by the Yugoslavs and he had no directive from the Italian government.

As a test, our captain said we would have a church parade of the Bluejackets, our improvised band, and 200 of our men. These would be joined by crews from the other destroyers, and, we were pleased to know, a contingent of Tommies from the Yorkshire and Lancashire regiment. They were just back from the Piave battlefield north of Trieste. There is always a feeling of brotherhood, a sort of affinity, when soldiers meet sailors in a foreign clime. They regularly visited us with their scratch military band, which had a young corporal for a conductor, and we would often have chats with them about Blighty. To us they were grand. Sunday morning arrived; we landed, all spick and span, unarmed and marched to a cinema theatre to hold the divine service. Arriving at 10.00 a.m. the cinema was nearly full of Italian soldiers and sailors watching a film.

---

[n] Gabriele D'Annunzio set up a Regency in Fiume with himself as Duce. The constitution made music the fundamental principle of the state and was corporatist in nature. Some of the ideas later influenced Italian fascism and Mussolini.

Fred on the left in a Postcard home from Fiume
Yugoslavia

Fiume 23-6-19   Fred Smith on left.

My Darling Louie.
A photo taken at   The boys names are
Spalato, Dalmatia
also two Jugo Slav boys   Drago Koracävic and
who were our interpreters
for my chum who's from   Amos Perkovantch
New Cross.
Tons of love and kisses
Always Yours dear
     Fred xxxxx
         xxxxx

172

They had defied our request. So we lined up outside. Our captain and army officers went inside and the film was stopped, which provoked the Italians to create a threatening din. We were ordered to march in, which we did. Then, after forcing the Italians away from front rows, we sat down and the Tommies' band went on the platform. There was uproar. However, our captain was quite cool and persistent as we sang the first hymn, Onward Christian Soldiers. Chosen, because it was easy to play and one of the few which the band knew. This seemed to have a subduing effect on the Italians, who quietened down. The service went on; prayers were said, followed by more hymns and then we left the cinema. Having cooled the ardour of the Italians, we marched through the main streets of Fiume playing old English marches such as Old Comrades and Colonel Bogey. We put on a smart show which must have impressed the populace.

Arriving back at our ship we parted company with the Tommies, who returned to their temporary billets. We thought, "So far so good." But the evening brought hostile demonstrations by hundreds of Italian civilians, military and naval personnel. So much so, that our gangways were hauled aboard and armed marines stood by at the ready, with torch lights. The Italians became very excited, especially when one of their airmen in a seaplane, a rare sight in those days, swooped dangerously low over us. Our captain ordered the Italian commander in chief to, "Cease this hostility; else the British may take action."

Meanwhile, the powers that be, had decided that Italy must evacuate Fiume, and gave an ultimatum to D'Ammunzio that he was to quit with the Italian army and navy by a specified date. We were reinforced by the battleship *Ajax*, our flagship *Cardiff* and some more destroyers.

The Italians remained defiant, and although a lot of their civilians were leaving in case of trouble, their fleet ignored the ultimatum. Twelve hours before the time limit, the Italian navy was warned to raise steam and leave Fiume, but then their crews mutinied and refused the order. As tension grew, it seemed that things might get out of hand. Thousands of Italians thronged the docks, and so two destroyers were detached to take off all our Tommies who were threatened by grenades. The destroyers were ordered to fix warheads to their torpedoes and load ammunition around their gun positions. *Cardiff* and *Ceres* did the same, all raising full steam and standing by. All the captains were alerted as to the plan of action. In front of us lay an Italian battle cruiser, the *Dante Aligheri*. We moved our position astern of her and sufficiently close, so that her twelve-inch guns could not be depressed low enough to hit us. We had eight twenty-one inch torpedoes, which were made ready under tarpaulins, in order to obscure what we were doing. As the night wore on, Italian sailors deserted their ships and began to mix with the excited crowd ashore. Nobody could sleep with the noise and all the excitement that was going on. We wondered what on earth would happen and, although apprehensive, we tried to remain calm and steady. We had them bottled up, but men driven to desperation can do such crazy things, and that coupled with treachery and hate...

The sun rose on what was, as far as nature was concerned, a glorious morning. Our destroyers slowly moved to their allotted positions and anchored in the middle of the dock basin, with their torpedoes trained on the Italian fleet and their crews at 'action stations'. Two Italian battleships were raising steam and preparing to leave the docks but the one lying ahead of us was still defiant, and so the tension rose. We had an early breakfast and made ready for trouble. The Italian civilians on the quay were threatening us, shouting insults and throwing things but we were ordered to ignore them, and their missiles.

The Italians were an excitable bunch, who did not like discipline, which was one of their failings. In this case, their bark was worse than their bite. An Italian General was sent to try and prevent hostile action and asked to observe the Armistice terms, but he was overruled by his Dictator or Patriot. The minutes ticked by and an Italian destroyer, together with merchant ships and transports, presumably with hundreds of civilians aboard, began leaving the dockside. Moving close by our destroyers they eventually steamed slowly out to sea. Stragglers were towed out by our English destroyers. However, the battleships stayed put and were a real problem. They were warned again. Whereupon the battleship, lying just ahead of us, suddenly fired a blank charge from her twelve-inch turrets on her stern, which went right over our heads. The blast was like an earthquake reverberating around the mountains in the quiet morning air. This started further excitement among the Italians on shore. As for myself, I was deafened, and thought I might have bitten my tongue through. Everyone was temporarily stunned by the concussion, and the flash had been terrific. The Italian captain of the battle cruiser was trying to maintain order and smoke was seen coming from his ship's funnels but he signalled that he could not get under way before the ultimatum had expired.

    Whereupon our captain sent an officer and seamen to prepare to take her in tow. They were jostled and hampered, but a stout wire hawser was made fast to our bows, mooring lines were let go and gangways put ashore. We took the boarding party aboard again and slipped our moorings. Down below, the signal sounded, 'slow astern', we waited and "Yes, we're moving!" We were only moving very slowly, owing to the ship's weight of about 20,000 tons. Slowly we towed her out past the *Cardiff* and a French cruiser and then out to the open sea. We set the battle cruiser adrift and left her to her own resources. There was no more defiance. But she could have blown us out of the water. I kept my fingers crossed as we returned to the docks, where the two remaining battleships were slipping their moorings and then slowly creeping out of the docks, ignominiously, as though in defeat. The populace were now subdued and very quiet. So, at 8 bells, 8.00 a.m., the ultimatum time, we raised our colours because all was well and bands played the National Anthem. A crisis had been averted.

    The Yugoslavs began to return to town with loads of flowers and wine, and they were a friendly crowd, blowing us kisses and dancing. A bugle sounded the 'secure', which meant that we could revert to normal and disarm our guns and torpedoes. Thank goodness they were not used, as the loss of life would have been terrible for both sides. It had been a case of our fellow's bluff outwitting the other fellow's bluff.

A fleet auxiliary arrived from Malta with stores, provisions, and mail from Blighty. There was a backlog of letters, with some ticking me off for not writing, which was not my fault, but the earliest dated one gave me a momentary, shall I say, shock! It was to change my life. Yes! I was to be a Daddy! I cannot quite say how I felt. What does one say when one acquires so much more responsibility, and on such sparse cash? But whatever betides, I will pull through. Events over the previous twenty-four hours, unbeknown to those at home, had been filling my mind but now, what a change in my thoughts. When I told my messmates they congratulated me and said I would have to, 'shove the boat out'. I said we must wait for the event and not be precipitate but promised that wherever we were in November 1919, I would keep my word.

I replied to the mail, full of congratulations and apologies for the pause in mail delivery. I expressed my delight and said that I was sorry I could not be with her. But I knew she had some good staunch friends, which eased my mind. Now worry had seemed a constant companion to me in my young life. I suppose it was my lot. At present we had no real home of our own and relied on Uncle Matt sharing his furniture. With no welfare services, like today, it was a case of get on with it and, again... just *hope*. Then I thought of my dear mother, how she had endured so much worse than us, and I knew my wife would face up to any trials that may come along. I was thousands of miles away, however, and oblivious of home conditions, where there was so much unemployment and scarcity of money. So I said, "The Lord will provide." Words I had learned from the Bible but I shall rely on *hope;* the word so many had given up thinking of. I resolved to be optimistic, live for the day and get down to my engineering studies.

I had been informed that I had been selected to go to an engineering college in England and possibly become an engineer lieutenant, if I proved satisfactory. This was a new Admiralty venture to promote from the lower decks. I was dead keen.

To revert to Fiume and the happenings ashore. Now that tension had eased, even the Italian garrison and the national

The Ship's Pet Lamb

Italian military police, the Carabiniers, were friendly disposed towards us. It seemed common sense had prevailed.

My messmates had purchased two monkeys, one very small, so small it could sit in one hand, and the other much bigger, more like an ape. They were great fun but destructive and mischievous, a term often applied to children. Another stoker had a tiny lamb. Feeding these animals was a problem but everyone on board helped. The monkeys had their own hammocks, according to their size, with small blankets but no pyjamas; anyway, we did not even have any of those luxuries. The owners trained them to go to bed in their own hammocks. The little one had such a funny face and would chatter away as though saying his prayers. They seemed to enjoy the fun of going ashore with the sailors and sometimes got tipsy with the boys. The lamb also got very knowing and very tame but, like its owner, it was rather sheepish and very dim!

On board, we settled down to an easy routine. I had a party of stokers whose job it was to clean the boilers, oil fuel tanks and to carry out double bottom jobs. These could be dangerous owing to the presence of inflammable gases and foul air, both of which could be deadly. Having had a thorough examination in the technique of working in confined spaces; it was deemed by the engineer commander that I would be the best petty officer for such jobs. I had always insisted that men should talk, sing or whistle while working in double bottoms or oil tanks. By that method, if I could hear them, I knew all was well. You see, the effect of foul air, would be an instant blackout. We only had one mishap. One morning the men went into a tank before I had thoroughly tested the air, which I did very often with a safety lamp. When I arrived at the tank and called out below, I received no answer. I summoned assistance and, with a line around my waist, went down, holding my breath, and there were my chaps, all unconscious, at the bottom. Ropes were lowered and with help, and in turns, I got them out into the fresh air. When they rallied, I gave them a dressing down for being over-zealous. After that, I had their implicit trust, so we were a happy team. And we were all getting nine-pence a day extra in danger money, but to us in those days nine-pence was a lot of money to us, believe me!

When mail had arrived, and while it was being read, silence reigned supreme. Some lads would receive grave news, others, gay news and maybe others, like me, were expecting news of a youngster on the way. Anyway, after reading the epistles, the lads' topics of conversation would be about mums, dads, wives, and sweethearts, and all at home. "Bless 'em all!" I say. Each shipmate would have his own story. Sometimes it would be a case of love turning to hatred, and if somebody had been jilted, judging by the jilted one's naughty nautical remarks, the lost girl's ears must surely have been burning.

Then my writing session would begin. I had learned that conditions at home were very bad. Unemployment and distress had taken over in the homeland in the aftermath of war. But my wife, bless her, was bravely carrying on and earning a few shillings. That is, until her pregnancy would forbid even that. In spite of the odds against us, we did not moan. We had both lived the hard way and learnt to grin and bear whatever may betide. Strains and stresses never altered our mutual love and respect. If anything, it made us more tolerant, trusting and understanding and may have moulded our characters. In this way we carried on our love at long distance, never reproachful and always cheery and each of us hiding any gloom. We would always write at the end of our letters, "Keep smiling dear."

Now, to change the subject and revert to my story. I went ashore many times at Fiume, seeing as many sights and people as I could. On one occasion, I climbed 900 steps. Yes, I counted them. I climbed up a small mountain where I was rewarded with a superb view of natural grandeur, something mankind is only too ready to disfigure, but there it was, a panorama of Fiume. And there, in the docks, the *Ceres* and *Cardiff* looking like toy boats floating on the ever-blue sea. "What's this Smudge, praise for the 'cruel sea'?" Around me I could see vineyards and orchards on the slopes, against a background of mountains, all in their natural beauty. From the ramparts of the Napoleonic fort, which I was standing in, I looked down a cascade of waterfalls, a sheer drop of six to seven-hundred feet.

Many Happy Returns of your Birthday 15-6-1919

Fred's Postcard to Louisa from Fiume

10 - 6 - 1919

My Darling Louie
            As I'm unable to get you a proper Birthday card I enclose you many Many Happy Returns of your Birthday and in Peace hoping I can wish you personally next year with some hearty kisses. Will this one do me good this year I'll TRY for you dearie. Always with tons of love and kisses Your ever loving
            Fred x x x x x x

These are leses boys and York & Lancs Regt.

I was overawed by the beauty of that place, and it is still something I remember today. It confirmed my belief in an invisible Master Architect. On descending, I went to a village amid the vineyards, were the people were happier, now that the Italians had been subdued. There, I was offered was wine, almonds and other fruits, while the girls, in their picturesque costumes, danced and sang. Even with their mean existence they seemed so happy. The sun was setting after a hot day and my white suit was wet in places with sweat but everyone else was the same, so it was no matter. I joined others on a stroll down from the peace and quiet, and back into the town with all the noise of cafés and servicemen getting high, silly, happy, boisterous and offensive. All of which would be soon be leading to quarrels galore. This is why, as often as possible, I would get away from the bars and out into the wilds; as it were. I went past the Yorkshire and Lancashire band playing in the square, with plenty of spectators around, and then back to *Ceres* and the sorting out of our money, Austrian kroners and filers. One had to be a mathematical genius with that fluctuating currency.

The next day, we were paraded in our best rigs for a special day. The Italian, French and English commanders in chief were holding a parade to foster friendly relations. The Tommies mustered in force, with the Royal Marines and, of course, our amateur band. We arrived at the main square where the Italian Bersaglieri° band was playing. The Italian soldiers were a scruffy slovenly crowd to behold and were in a sultry mood, while the British lads gave a wonderful show of smartness and discipline. We all felt very glad to be taking part in this special occasion and were duly inspected and commended on our appearance. The Marines, especially the leathernecks, certainly showed that they knew their stuff. At the request of the Italian commander in chief, the Marines did some small-arms drill and, as usual, they were very precise, in fact they looked perfect to me. The Royal Marines always seemed to me to be "perfection at its finest." The

---

° Bersaglieri - light infantry unit with a fast jog pace on parades and wide brimmed hats decorated with black feathers.

surrounding crowds agreed and showed their appreciation. We returned with the band and our white ensign to our ships, where our mess-decks smelt of the rose perfume which had been given to us by the Yugoslav girls. The twang of our oil fuel had, for once, been overcome!

The next morning brought arrears of mail and newspapers, so we had plenty of reading and writing. The news from Louisa was reassuring; my brother George was back in his job on the electric trams as a conductor. But apparently back at home, there was a scarcity of jobs and food, which was not a happy thought, considering that we had won the War.

We prepared for sea again and as we steamed from the Fiume dockside the Yugoslavs gave us a rousing goodbye.

A post card Fred sent home from Fiume

Chapter 21 – Summer in Malta

In glorious weather we steamed south at twenty knots making for Malta. The only discomfort was the cockroaches; we had swarms of them on board. As we lay in our hammocks, dreaming of home, some lads playing mandolins, life seemed ideal, but if we touched the deck above our heads we would sweep hundreds of these beastly cockroaches into our hammocks. Then we would have to get out of bed and shake our bedding to get rid of these pests.

We were approaching the heel of Italy and were due to call in at Taranto for a courtesy visit, and we were due to have one night ashore. It was an interesting port with gay music and cafés along the waterfront but it was only a very brief visit and then off we went the next day to Malta. Burnt Malta, with temperatures in the eighties, and in our boiler room, around 120 degrees. At that temperature we had to slow our movements down, so as not to sweat too much, but we still had to wear the thick clothing on our legs to protect us from the furnace heat. But it was a case of "What keeps the heat out, will keep it in" Like many other things, we got used to it. Air at 80 degrees, forced down from the upper decks, was cool to us. The ship being oil-fired meant our work was not laborious. My duty was regulating the oil temperature and pressure, and making all necessary adjustments. When going at a steady speed, one could easily regulate things and time would pass along until the evening. Then things would turn very humid and sultry and sleep would be difficult. I would lie there sweating, wondering and planning all sorts of things and thinking of family, friends, Louisa, and... a little stranger! So long as one had no worries, all was well.

One night there was an electrical storm with an unusual amount of sheet lightning, which, without any thunder, lit up the whole dark night sky with bluish flashes. It was all very pretty. The ship's rigging crackled with static electricity and the effect on the sea was magical. It was fascinating to watch: as the ship glided along our bow wave was lit up with a bluish white illumination; where the hull met the water one could see a band of phosphorescence and at the stern the wake of the screws made beautiful white glowing spirals. Even the fishes, large and small, would be glowing, while the porpoises played, as is their wont, leaping out of the water and displaying their luminous bellies.

This sort of thing is so awe inspiring and grand that it makes one wonder about the technique and skills which Mother Nature uses for such displays. Yes, she can be contrary and at times drive sailors to distraction and curses, but not that night. Was it meant to persuade us to change our minds, and to lead us to appreciate some of the lovely things, even if only for brief spells, that Mother Nature and the Creator can provide? Little sleep was had by all of those who were lucky enough to be off duty that night but when eight bells came, 4 a.m., I was on watch again.

Finishing my watch, I found that we were steaming towards the Grand Harbour at Malta to have a minor refit and machinery overhaul. There is a naval ritual associated with entering harbours: there was the *Cardiff*, with the Admiral aboard, all her ship's crew lining the rails and wearing their whites, the guns on forts ashore fired an 'admiral's salute', bands played and ensigns flew as we slowly entered the harbour. What a majestic sight. Other ships lined up, also in ceremonial fashion. It all made one proud of the British navy and there was no one prouder than me.

As we tied up to buoys we could revert to our normal Maltese routine, with no more washing up dishes at mealtime, because the Maltese boys would do all that. Leaving their Dhaisos – their small boats for selling wares. These Maltese were professional and persistent cadgers and loveable rogues, because they were so very ingenious.

We had orders to go into dry-dock to have the *Ceres* bottom cleaned, under-water fittings over-hauled and the whole ship painted a light grey. Storerooms were replenished and a refrigeration plant was installed with more air-conditioning. Evening time was enchanting with mandolins and banjos playing on the Dhaisos, which looked just like gondolas, as they were rowed in a similar method, with the oars being pushed.

Food was uninviting ashore owing to lavish use of olive oil, which in hot weather was not palatable. I did not want their frills, just plain food: bacon, eggs, chops or fish and chips. I visited some museums and the 'chapel of bones', which was a small church with walls and an altar festooned with human bones. It was gruesome but an interesting place. There were gardens with oranges, limes and lemons growing in profusion, but it was without the green grass of England. By day the sun would cause a terrific glare as it reflected on the limestone buildings, and the natural puce colour of the earth. People without sunglasses had to keep their eyes practically closed for comfort.

Preparations began to celebrate Peace Day which was planned for July 19th 1919. We got everything ready and started the day early. The *Ceres* was lying in Grand Harbour, all spick and span and looking her best. At eight bells, 8 a.m., with our band playing the National Anthem, the colours were hoisted. There was the 'Jack' flying at our stern with a silk white Ensign, which was so long it nearly touched the water. The order was 'dress ship', which meant strings of bunting being hoisted from bow to top mast, mizzen and stern, whilst white canvas awnings were put up to shelter decks from mid-day sun. We received another signal telling us that a divine service in the assembled fleet would take place. At two bells, 9.00 a.m, all the ships' companies paraded on their quarterdecks. A couple of hymns were sung and the captain said prayers followed by the National Anthem being sung. It must have been a memorable sight, simple but impressive. Ashore all was quiet, except for the church bells calling the Maltese to their cathedral and churches.

After church parade, we were dismissed for the day, and I went ashore, after dinner, with a lot of the lads by Dhaiso. The afternoon was hot, so I went bathing in Beka Bay, a lovely silver sandy beach. The clear warm water was so nice, if only to sit in up to my neck to keep cool. That was a rarity for me, as I do not like swimming, especially when the water is cold. I envy others who revel in it but I cannot. But I could not resist this place, so calm and warm. I was able to see my floating home, so lovely in all her splendour. Then evening arrived and the din and noise in the cafés and pubs became terrific. The buglers sounded 'sunset' when all the service men stood to attention, facing the white ensign. This is another naval ritual worth seeing, although perhaps some would say it is just a silent tribute to a bit of rag. Darkness speedily followed, and the illuminations were switched on, picking out the outlines of all the ships in thousands of electric lights. What a gasp there was from all the people ashore, especially when the searchlights were switched on turning night into day. My mate and I, not wanting to frequent pubs, had a quiet supper and strolled around watching sailors and soldiers thoroughly enjoying themselves, and some, especially the single ones, getting very drunk. As I never slept ashore, it was time to return aboard. We climbed into a Dhaiso and to the sound of music from the cafes ashore, we were slowly rowed back to the *Ceres*. She was an 'old girl' now, but I still loved her.

After a few more days we steamed out of Grand Harbour on our own and proceeded north through the Straits of Messina, past the volcanic island of Stromboli, where, in the evening gloom, one could see fire and smoke around the volcano's crater, which, it is said, is always fiery. Still going north, we steamed up the Italian coast pass the Isle of Elba, after which we ran into a storm and the sea became rough. When steaming through the Ligurian Sea we were pitching and rolling rather badly, which was quite a nasty change because it brought back my Atlantic memories, but, thank goodness, it only lasted for one day.

We sighted the Riviera coast, quite close to Nice, which was looking very picturesque with its white casinos and yachts lying at anchor in a calm blue sea. Behind the town, one could see rising slopes and hills covered with greenery. We sailed on along the Riviera coast, passing Monte Carlo and eventually arriving at Marseilles. There we anchored close enough to the shore, and stayed long enough, to give the ship's company a chance to land in France.

Marseilles is a shipping port with extensive docks and, like our own docklands, plenty of drab and squalid houses making it quite different from Nice. The cathedral of Notre Dame overlooks the town and seafront of cafés with their gaily coloured tables on the pavement. There, one could indulge in a little refreshment of Vin Rouge or Vin Blanc. One drink was sufficient, as it tasted like insipid vinegar to me. The French have wine with every meal. For my part they are welcome to it, I would rather have an English cup of tea! I cannot say I was fascinated with the town but the visit was very brief with no time for anyone to get into mischief.

After our captain and officers had been entertained by the civic authorities, we weighed anchor and sailed away on a straight course for Gibraltar, where we hoped, if we would were lucky, we would have news from home. For the postal service, it was like a game of 'hide and seek', because we were never in one place for very long, and letters would accumulate, giving us a problem to sort out. The weather was unbelievably sublime, so warm and sunny, and as we cruised at eighteen knots it was perfect for doing our hobbies and games on the upper deck. Bingo or Housey-Housey, as we called it, was popular for ha'penny a game. Although gambling, as such, was forbidden, this was permissible.

Chapter 22 – Gibraltar

On our way south-west we passed Majorca and in due course we reached the Spanish coast which was on our starboard beam. We hugged the coast and when we had steamed 1400 miles from Malta we arrived at the Rock of Gibraltar. It looked like a couchant lion guarding the Straits and to the South, the faint outline of North Africa. The Rock itself is about 1300 feet high and has a small town and dockyard. We anchored in the bay with Algeciras to the West, what a lovely panorama, with the Rock looking so forbidding.

We were there for some new equipment and so were moved inside the dockyard with other naval units, and some submarines. I had always wanted to board a submarine and I thought this would be my chance.

And yes, there was a large mail delivery for us. That always got the lads in a serious mood, me included. I hoped for news of how Louisa was faring with her, 'new experience'. All was well, except that *now* I had to answer five or six letters from her. I would usually reply to letters as, and when, they arrived but I was constantly being ticked off from home for not writing often enough. However, at sea we had no daily postman knocking on our door. Important items of news were exchanged amongst the crew, and, yet again, if they could hear the lads' jokes and remarks, wives and sweethearts back home would surely feel their ears burning. I would be greeted by, "How's the old woman Smudge?"

"So-So," I would say, "and that's your lot."

Gibraltar was typically English, except for the 'Rock Scorpions' as the Spanish work people were called. To the north of Gibraltar was a strip of flat land, about a mile in depth and width, a peninsula, called the Neutral Ground. It had customs posts either end and a race course and sports grounds in between. In the morning there would be the ceremony of keys, when the governor, with escort and band, would open the frontier gate admitting the Spanish workmen who had passes. When they returned home at night, a gun would be fired, which would be the signal for locking the gate. Looking up, the steep side of the Rock was studded with guns to repel any attack from the landward side. In fact, the whole Rock bristled with heavy guns facing seawards as well, and that was why it was considered impregnable. The Rock was a honeycomb of tunnels, and had a cable railway to take stores and provisions to the garrison quartered near the top. There was no water problem there, because the eastern slope was cemented on its very steep side to catch the rain, which then flowed to an underground reservoir, and when it rained on the Rock, it just literally fell down.

The shops at sea level were interesting. Many of the private residences were windowless with slats fitted instead. The reason for this was that when the heavy guns were being used for firing exercises, the concussion would smash any glass to smithereens. The populace were given due warning of firings and all their doors and windows would be left open.

It was here that my pal and I indulged in a glass of real port wine. A glass cost just tuppence, and one glass each made my mate Bob and I tipsy. So we had to keep out of the way of the other lads or we would not have lived it down. It certainly was potent and cheap, but, as I have said, we watched our expenses, and tried not to be foolish and waste money. Feeling 'muzzy', we made our way to the Alemeda Gardens, which looked quite natural with a profusion of flowering shrubs and other exotic plants. Being a hundred feet above the town a beautiful view was to be had of the sunlight, in the clear air, shining over the sea. We had a little siesta, a custom in these parts after dinner, and a custom I have acquired and still enjoy to this day.

How I now like to relive those times and that tranquil scene, with the singing of the birds, the distant strains of banjos and guitars from down in the town and not a worry, or care, in the world.

One of the interesting features on the Rock was the apes which lived on the slopes. Notices in places of prominence warned the public not to feed the apes owing to their nuisance value, and, of course, their tendency to be destructive. They are not aggressive, and steal down the old Moorish walls to chatter and hope that someone will give them some titbits. As we sat in the gardens we were really amused by these apes' antics. They were so interesting we decided to go higher up, into their haunts. So, a day or two later, we bought a quantity of nuts and climbed up the rock for about 600 feet and settled down in a comfortable spot. We could see some houses, which were soldiers' family homes. The wives had a trying time when drying their washing and a sentry had to be posted to scare off the monkeys, sorry I mean apes, but the sentry was forbidden to kill any, as the apes would have had their revenge, because, like elephants, they are supposed, never to forget. The apes would ransack the dwellings if they gained admittance, so preventive measures were vital. We saw the apes in the trees doing all sorts of trapeze acts. Parent apes were instructing their youngsters how to swing using their hands, feet and tails and chattering away all the time, and completely ignoring us. The mums would suckle their babes at their breasts while dads would look on with grimaces. At a rough count, I suppose this colony had about fifty or sixty old and young apes. We were fascinated because they were so much like us humans. The elderly males had beards and some were nearly as big as I was, well, I am of a slight build! Young apes would be swung by their tails from tree to tree, squealing, and then be caught by another of the apes. Their faces were so funny.

    So, in this ideal weather, Bob and I just lazed in the sun, whilst watching the fun. We got out some nuts and enticed them to join us, maybe we should not have done that, but they seemed docile enough. Gradually they gathered around us like we were all in a family circle – but Bob and I could be distinguished from the apes by our white caps and blue collars! As we threw nuts to them, they seated themselves quite close. We refrained from stroking them in case the senior ones attacked us. There they were, all chattering away, the old and young, mums and babies, when Bob said, "Come on folks what about a song." It was quite a party that everyone was enjoying, until the nuts ran low. I was aware of a big hairy arm over my shoulder trying to snatch the nuts from my jumper. I held its hand, which was as big as my own, and studied the lines on it. I nudged Bob and said, "What now, Bob?"

"Blimey Smudge, watch out!" When I looked, what a scare I had; this very large ape, with his flowing beard, appeared to be resenting me pulling his arm and was showing his teeth. At this scary moment a Spaniard passed by and I asked, "Hey Jose, what do we do?"

"Just get up and walk away, yes?" He answered, waving his hand. But our first attempt to leave failed as we were pulled back down. So, with some little trepidation, we scattered the rest of the nuts, got up and departed. The apes became very excited but kept their distance. Having had quite a scare, we scrambled down the steep rock. The apes mounted the wall and slid down on their bottoms following us. We eventually came to the Moorish wall, built by the Moors from Africa years ago, and while the apes watched us from above, they ventured no further, and we were relieved to get among humans again.

Now, for a cup of tea and something to eat while we watched the passing show of Gibraltarian life. The Spanish men and women added colour to the scene with their national mode of dress, black tresses, and their brown oily skins. We sat and studied the fashions and after tea, watched a fiesta, of Spanish dancing, with castanets and mandolins. It was a free concert in the open air. Some service men would join in until they were bathed in sweat and would have to retire. There was a cooling breeze from the sea and we could watch the shipping passing to and fro.

I watched a big liner coaling from a collier, which revived memories of that filthy hard work on my previous ships. Now the sun was setting and bathing the Rock in an orange glow. The cafés were livening up with music and dancing. It was worth pausing here to watch the scene change and the setting sun throw the Rock in relief, showing it off at its best. We had an 'all night leave' and so put up at a Salvation Army Hostel where we had a good rest.

As I have said, when it rained there, it was very heavy. The streets would be deserted and, if caught out, one would get soaked. Once would be enough! If there was a possibility of rain, we would flock back to ship, as it persisted all day. In the dock we were having our armament modified and air conditioning improved. We could enjoy reading the latest news, although from the homeland it was dismal, with much unemployment and many shortages. The news was causing concern on board, but we could do nothing about it. Letters from home were always cheerful, in spite of the privations families must have been enduring. So we tried to put it out of our minds.

I satisfied my curiosity and had my visit aboard a submarine, seeing their inner mysteries, cramped living conditions and masses of machinery all packed into such a tiny space.

I thoroughly enjoyed my visit to Gibraltar and it is always a pleasure to remember it.

We had our sailing orders and so took on a supply of oil, the smell permeating the whole ship. Then we were towed out of the dock and made ready to leave. Our band together with the soldiers' band ashore played lively music, while everyone gave lusty cheers which marked the breaking of temporary friendships.

We steamed away due east into an open sea. Slowly the Rock faded into the distance and eventually there was neither land nor a cloud in sight. We settled down to our watch-keeping, our daily routines and occasionally dipping our ensign as a liner from the Far East passed us. In response, by the code of seafarers, they would dip their flag in salute, a simple but friendly gesture.

We neared the African coast and passing Algiers we could feel the hot breezes from the Sahara Desert. The temperature by day was in the nineties and a cold bath was a luxury. Life in the boiler and engine rooms, as you may imagine, was anything but pleasant and we always had to be careful in handling anything metallic. Everything was very hot but we managed alright with the help of draughts of iced-water and by keeping ourselves near the huge fans. Sleeping on the upper deck was the rule, as the speed of the ship would create a breeze and ease the conditions.

We were nearing Malta and began wondering if there would be mail from home awaiting us. Moored once again in the Grand Harbour we found out that we have received a special mission; a suite of cabins aft were prepared and decorated for 'royal personage and retinue'. "Who might this be?" We wondered. I went ashore several times, just looking around, but could only visit in the late afternoon as mid-day was so very warm. Evening time was the best, when and the cool breezes and music made a happy memory.

Chapter 23 – Autumn in Turkey

After a couple of weeks we were off to sea again. This time bound for Constantinople, about 880 miles from Malta. We steamed through the Grecian Archipelago, which were lovely islands spread out on either side of us. It was so calm that it was possible to see the bottom of sea, which was covered in plant life of lovely colours, and we could watch all the fish swimming around. When we stopped at Lemnos we saw octopuses on the rocks below us and Greek fishermen diving down and bringing some to the surface. The octopuses were not huge but I understand they were a delicacy.

We left Lemnos and steamed north to the Dardanelles, where we anchored in a very narrow strip of water, with a swift current. It was the scene of the Gallipoli fighting a few years earlier. It was truly a desolate spot. There we were, with Europe on one side and Asia on the other. We then steamed east spotting various places of wartime interest such as the forts, many of which were now in ruin. We then reached the narrows where the current was even stronger. Very close by, on either side, there were formidable coastlines. After the narrows we came to the Sea of Marmora, which was a very tranquil stretch of water with beautiful scenery on our port beam. Eventually we arrived at Constantinople, now called Istanbul. It was a hot day and we could tell by the aroma floating on the breeze that we were nearing a city. From our position, west of city, the view was very interesting, with mosques and minarets. We dropped anchor in the Golden Horn, where many ships of foreign nationalities were assembled. We were saluted by the other ships dipping their ensigns and bands playing the National Anthem.

Now to take stock. The city was a wonderful panorama of numerous blue domed mosques and minarets, and, with the Sultan's Palace, it all made a colourful picture. We were to be there for a few days but were warned of the danger of going ashore singly. However, our Tommies were there and, again, if we obeyed the rules and stayed alert, all should be well. We found the Turks received us very coolly, and the streets were very narrow, cobbled and uneven, with garbage and litter rampant. Pariah dogs were everywhere searching for food and the smell was pungent and nauseating. Sanitary systems seemed to be unknown. It was a good job we had been inoculated against typhus, dysentery and typhoid, because they were prevalent there.

Now about the people we saw. Women were not emancipated at that time. They wore long robes, usually black, and down to ground level, and their faces were covered by yashmaks, with only their grey eyes showing. The men wore loose fitting clothes with their trouser bottoms situated at their knees. Practically all had praying mats slung on their backs. There was nothing gay about their dress and their homes were even worse, being made of wood chiefly. When a fire started, it usually meant a whole street went up in flames, and to stop it spreading, houses would be blown up to make a fire-gap. At all hours, from early morning till dusk, a Muezzin would call the faithful to prayer from high up on the minarets. That would be when all Muslims, wherever they were, in wet or fine weather, would put their mats down, face the east, and do all sorts of contortions in a very serious mood and, by banging their foreheads on the ground during their prayers, would get filthy. Of course, we dared not make fun and smile, in case there was trouble. This was a city of contrasts, where obscenity, vice and holy devotion seemed close neighbours. It had to be seen to be believed. Veritably, it was a den of iniquity and showed how low morals can really get. To be on the streets or, worse still, in the alleyways after dark was a certain danger. So, safety first, we stayed aboard at night. But I was determined to see all I could during our stay. One day a party of us decided to go into the old city of Istanbul, which was a hot bed of intrigue and religion. Going through the main street we boarded a tram, which we discovered had three compartments, one curtained off for Muslim women. Next a compartment for devout Muslim men, and then the riff-raff and infidels, which included us! We had to stand at the back with all the natives, some of whom were lousy and unkempt and, as it was hot, the smell was... but, thank goodness, it was not a long ride. We alighted at a floating bridge, which rose and fell a little with the tide. The Mediterranean is practically tide-less. We entered Istanbul with the Mosque of St. Sophie facing us. A Moslem offered to show us inside and we had to remove our shoes and leave them in the doorway before we could go inside. It was very luxurious with lots of tapestries, gold and silver. There were no seats and the floor was made of marble where there were many worshippers kneeling and praying, while someone, somewhere, was chanting mournfully in Arabic. Of course, I did not know what it was all about but I tried to appear serious, knowing where we were and to be polite to our guide. Our visit inside over, we returned to the street, and, yes, our shoes were still there because they were in a holy place.

 Will I ever understand how people of different religions behave or who is right? This mosque must have cost a fortune; it was so lavish, with its jewels, marble and precious metals. We were fascinated by this visit but then turned to the bazaar, which is a place of worldwide fame. Our Tommies had warned us never to go into the bazaar alone, so we kept together whilst watching craftsmen with ivory and ebony doing exquisite inlaid work. There were lace makers, rug makers, and turkish delight as only Turks can make it. The narrow alleys, the very old buildings and the arcades, were sights to see!

 The Turkish gendarmes were numerous because of the number of thieves. A theft always caused an exciting rumpus and was fun, to watch. Then we came across something that seemed out of this world: a real scribe, an old man with flowing robes, beard and fez, who looked like something from the Bible. Here he was, in a crude market place, with a native customer kneeling on the ground saying his piece, while he wrote a letter with a quill pen on a roll of parchment, writing the native's words in Arabic, which looked like wriggling worms to me. If only I had a camera with me for a snapshot. This place seemed to hark back centuries. Women were rarely seen, and the few we did see, completely hid their faces. Yet, I believe the women were beautiful with grey steely eyes. Muslims would sit in the road smoking through a hookah, a hubble-bubble pipe, a means by which more than one person can smoke, and the smoke passing through water. Many would be asleep, or doped, in the alleys. Sometimes the smell was awful, it was no wonder there was disease of all sorts. However, we carried on exploring because we wanted our fill of curiosity. Some Turks carried flowers, no doubt because the sweet scent of the roses soothed the nose amidst that garbage and filth. I will not mention their lavatories, save to say that they were awful and your need would have to be extremely urgent.

However, after this interlude we went back to the city and visited the English town, a part of the city called Pera, where shops had names such as Boots, and Singers. They were places where English was spoken. What a breath of fresh air that was. We bought some English tea, with English cakes and some other English items. We also learned of other places of interest, which it was suggested we should see if time permitted. To get to this colony we had to go through what was the most disgusting, filthy vice ridden area. It had a half a mile of brothels inhabited by women and girls of all nationalities, and all ages from twelve years of age to old women. Their appearance was deplorable, and their conditions were worse than cattle live in. I am pleased to say that none of our lads was tempted. How on earth could such a place exist in such a famous city as Constantinople? With regard to commercial transport, it was rather medieval, with mules, carts, and some traders using men as carriers. They would have a pad fixed on their haunches and would be loaded up. There would be perhaps ten men in a convoy, moving in a line at a steady pace, with ten sacks between them, making around a ton of goods in all. We thought that it was funny to see a Turk from a portmanteau, a suitcase shop, who had a framework of battens so that his cases were fixed in front of him, behind him, both sides and above his head, it was really comical.

Any purchases were made with piastres and we would bargain by writing the amount with a pencil, using numerals, which are, seemingly, universally understood. We, of course, avoided back alleys where the homes were very mediocre and filthy.

On another day, for a change of scene, we went east of the City along the Bosphorus to Dohna Batchie, the Sultans Palace and the Harem buildings, and what a contrast this was. Built of marble and white stone, it had wonderful gardens, which could only be seen from the outside as no visitors were allowed. One got a new smell here of roses from the rose gardens. Everywhere there were signs of wealth. Looking east across the swift flowing Bosphorus towards Therapia, there were hilly slopes and trees, where one could see the wealthy Turks' villas. This was a gorgeous sight, and so different from looking towards the west.

Being a polygamous country a man's harem might have several wives, or concubines. One could observe perhaps twelve women in gaily-coloured silken garments, and yashmaks, squatting on the grass making a colourful scene. It was said the Sultan's harem might have as many as a hundred wives and concubines. To us that seemed a very strange custom, but that was the pattern of life in Turkey at that time. We spent the day in an atmosphere of perfume and tidy well-made streets.

So much for Constantinople. We weighed anchor, but before we could go east, in order to be able to turn around, we had to steam west into the Sea of Marmora, because there was a ten-knot current in the narrows. Having turned around we steamed eastwards and were told that if we fell overboard we were to swim against the current, not with it. The current would then keep one's head up.

Passing through the Bosphorus we steamed east across an open sea. This was the Black Sea where the weather was warm, in fact, very hot, about 100 degrees in the shade. We steamed 600 miles to Batum, a small port in Georgia, which is part of Russia and near to Persia. We were surrounded by beautiful mountains with slopes covered in tea plantations and large orchards of limes, oranges, lemons and figs. The atmosphere of spice was very pleasant indeed. We moored to a wooden jetty where we had a lovely view of the beach. It is hard to describe in writing, but I will try. Awaiting us was a military guard of Russian Cossacks, armed with swords, knives, pistols and rifles – a veritable arsenal, I thought – but they were courteous towards us.

Now, this place seemed to be so perfect we called it Arcadia[p], because as far as one could see, there was a broad expanse of clean white silver sand which went on for miles, with just a few humble dwellings. Then there was the backcloth of mountains, their slopes studded with colourful vineyards and rose gardens. The roses here were grown for the manufacture of the perfume called Attar of Roses. The sea was a beautiful blue and so smooth, but with a perfect six foot surf wave all along the beach. We strolled along in our whites and then, to our amazement we saw, hundreds of Russian and Turkish people sunbathing in their 'birthday suits'. There were the young, old, beautiful and the not so beautiful. I rubbed my eyes wondering if I was dreaming. Some were swimming, some playing and some just wandering about in an apparently normal way. It struck me that we must have been the abnormal ones.

It was so hot that we decided to have a dip ourselves, so sat down, undressed and put on our, mostly dark blue, one-piece swimming costumes. My word the curiosity we caused. Young women came to see what we were wearing. Oh dear, were we embarrassed, or at least I was, seeing these lovely sun-tanned bodies of the young women. For us young sailors this was really something to remember for all our days! Being born in a conventional country, like Old England, we thought we would be immodest if we took our trunks off, in case we gave offence, so we carried on in our 'English fashion', which was much to the ladies amusement.

When our officers realized the situation on the beach, with this sort of custom, civilization took over and the beach was portioned off, with the natives at one end, the lower decks at the opposite and the officers in the middle! This was, I suppose, because the officers were to be trusted to behave correctly. I

---

[p] Arcady: Idealized rural setting in Greek and Roman poetry.

wonder! In the late afternoon, we had a stroll, after having got dressed, and meandered around the vineyards and other places, eating grapes and various other fruits. There was a light breeze blowing as we gazed upon the setting sun playing all sorts of tricks and changing the colours and shades of the beautiful scenery. Hence I had the idea of calling this place, Arcadia.

   I managed three visits ashore before our Royal guests arrived. They were His Majesty the Shah of Persia and members of his Government, all of whom were wearing jewelled fezzes. They were piped aboard the *Ceres* and the Persian standard was flown at the main. Our band did not know their National Anthem so that was dispensed with. We made ready for sea again, and this time steamed westward.

   We were at that time about 3,800 miles from home so had to remember to write, in order that our letters should be ready for collection. At times, however, because of our movements the mail deliveries were haywire.

   The Shah was a very rotund young man and our ships upper structure had to be modified to give his personage room for manoeuvre. He wanted to see everything and we had to keep him amused. We carried out high-speed battle practice at sea, with our five and six inch guns really making a noise. Torpedoes were fired, but with dummy warheads and, when it was dark, star-shells were fired, lighting up the sea vividly.

   My duties at this time included looking after the refrigeration plant on the upper deck and I had to keep making ice for the wardroom. The Persians would make me understand by gestures if they wanted an ice-drink. For this duty I managed to get some silver coins as a memento of their company.

   Steaming through the Bosphorus to Constantinople I find very difficult to describe. The timing was all arranged for the Shah's benefit and it was so grand. As we approached the city the rising sun in the east lit the mosques and minarets, all, of which were topped with turquoise and gold, and made all the grander by standing in relief against the dark blue dawn. It was truly a magical spectacle and a sight which I knew I would never see again. All ships in harbour were anchored with their bows facing the east as we steamed into the Sea of Marmora to turn around and anchor in the Golden Horn. We then discharged our royal visitors, with a royal salute from our guns, as they bid us farewell. Then we took different visitors aboard who were naval and military officers. We also managed to get a real load of mail, and get ours off to England. And there was one of my letters reminding me to expect some exciting news around about November.

Our stay was brief, without leave and we soon steamed east again and the next day arrived at Sebastopol in the Crimea, where the Russian Revolution was at its height. We anchored close to town. Afternoon leave was granted and were able to go ashore to see some sites, including a museum built on the place of the last Russian stand in the Crimean War. It was a circular building with a viewing platform in the middle. Over the whole interior of the wall was a panorama, as seen by eyewitness at the time of the Siege of Sebastopol. Where the canvas met the earth it blended in with the actual dugouts, with some of the sand bags, and even the earth, undisturbed. Dead soldiers' boots were still visible above the blood stained earth, and old cannons, some of which were real and some painted. It was so good, and very realistic, that it was hard to detect the real from painted. The daylight was diffused by muslin, making it seem a sacred place on top of the hill. Going to a higher platform one could look out of the windows and see the hills and harbour and it all matched with the painting. One would think that the men in the painting bleeding from wounds were real, as you would the British soldiers, who were depicted in the distance advancing from the Heights of Alma[a] near Balaclava.

The Russians were very passive and solemn towards us. They showed no gaiety at all and received us very casually. Some Russian naval destroyers were lying half-submerged in the harbour; sunk by the Bolsheviks.

---

[a] The Battle of Alma in the Crimean War 20th Sep 1854 Crimea, Ukraine.

Money was a problem so we did not change too much. We would share a pound's worth of roubles between us because each day the rate of exchange varied. A Jew volunteered to interpret for us, which was a relief, but we had to watch him very carefully. Then one night, in darkness, we raised our anchor and slipped away without lights. We steamed along the coast and anchored off a small town where we landed the officers, who had boarded earlier. They were secret agents, who landed disguised as Russians. We returned to Sebastopol and awaited a signal to return to pick up the agents, who were possibly trying to pick up some Russian companion loyalists. When undercover movements were in progress strict secrecy was to be observed and we could only surmise what intrigue was going on. Destroyers around the Crimea were also engaged in these cloak and dagger operations, which were all under cover of darkness. In Sebastopol, the Russians seemed uncertain as to their position and appeared subdued with not many smiles. We dared not stray away from the town, for we were soon to proceed on to Alexandria, in Egypt.

When we did set off again the weather was still sunny and warm as we steamed at twenty knots through the Grecian archipelago. But we were diverted to Malta, yet another alteration of plans, to re-stock with fuel and provisions and also to pick up our mail, which, as usual, was haywire. When we got it, I was quietly ticked off for not writing often enough, to Louisa.

We were back to the "bells, gels yells, and smells" of Malta to while away a few more days at leisure, but we soon learned that we had another VIP mission. Fully stocked and fuelled we steamed east again for another thousand miles to Port Said, where we tied up at moorings opposite the Suez Canal Main Office, to await our visitor.

Chapter 24 – Africa

Leave was granted and I landed on African soil. A port of call for all nationalities but, oh, what a place for slums and squalor, with plenty of beggars who pestered us incessantly with cheap merchandise and obscene postcards. A lot spoke Pidgin English, which we could understand but found very funny and quaint. I had a ride in a tram with no top deck and no sides. The seats were hard and went across the tram and one just scrambled aboard. They had a native driver controlling the tram's mules and a boy conductor who had a horn to warn the driver to 'stop' or 'go'. But the tram would only move if the mules agreed. We paid for things with piastres. The coins had holes in the centre, so that people could string them up and hang their wealth either around their necks or waist. Clothing was of poor quality and fit, and some went practically naked.

I had my first experience of the desert, with its endless stretches of hot sand and temperatures of 100 degrees in the shade. When the sun set, which was a wonderful sight in the desert, we had to change into a blue suit for warmth because nights seemed so cold after the burning day. Our pet monkeys were happy here among the date palms which grew near the town. The dates hung in bunches, like large damsons, and were blue and black in colour, and not brown, as I had known them at home.

My one regret is that I did not see Cairo or the Pyramids, but had to be satisfied with archaeologists digging at some local ruins, although this was very interesting. Arriving back in Port Said, we had tea, and ordered eggs and chips, which consisted of six small eggs and yams, a kind of sweet potato fried in olive oil. It was very greasy but we had to eat. When it was my turn to stay on board I would watch the natives, men and women, loading the ships with coal in baskets on their heads, whilst a chief Sarang, or foreman, with a cane kept them on the move. Dress seemed unimportant to them and they swore in English, appearing ignorant as to its meaning and so were unashamed. They also did not seem to care who was watching when they wanted to relieve nature's needs. The coaling was one constant procession of natives running up long planks and chanting monotonously all the time. Hundreds of natives would work nonstop on one liner until it was finished.

Port Said was reputed to be the fastest port for coaling ships, and was really a busy one, with large ships flying to and from the Far East through the Suez Canal. One morning we prepared to receive our VIP, Lord Allenby. The troops ashore formed a guard of honour and when the usual ceremonial concluded he was brought aboard the *Ceres* by a whaler and his staff followed. The reception over, we prepared for sea and steamed northward hugging the Palestinian coast in glorious weather until we arrived off Beirut. Landing was difficult owing to the surf and rocks. From the shore, a boat put out to warn us that there was an outbreak of typhus ashore. I was not surprised judging by the bad state of the town's sanitation, which smelt like rotting vegetation. It appears that Lord Allenby was to land and hand Beirut over to the French authorities. We could see French and British Tommies mustered ashore under the Union Jack, and so it was decided to hand the port over from on board the *Ceres*. Guns boomed ashore for a general salute and after the ceremony was concluded, the Union Jack was lowered and the French tri-colour hoisted in its place, while the French national anthem; the Marseilles was played. Then we awaited events.

Small boats loaded us with Jaffa oranges, lovely specimens and only two shillings for fifty. Also we had other, chiefly citrus, fruit. The limejuice was delicious, being the real juice. Bumboats came alongside selling all sorts of goods, some of which were phony. Fancy them trying to sell us pieces of the real cross on which Christ was crucified. Well, my comment on this was that the cross must have been very large! But I did buy a book of pressed flowers, with each page of the book from a holy place. How I wished I could have landed and visited those places. So near yet, at present, forbidden. We returned to Port Said with Lord Allenby and his staff, and tied up near the quay where we were to spend some days. This meant that I was able to get around the city. It was a rather a drab place, I thought, but it was amazing how people survived in such conditions, which were pitiful in the extreme. The natives were living like animals. Only animals, I think, sometimes have better morals than many humans. Drink and vice seemed the most noticeable feature here.

Visitors from liners were of every nationality and when making purchases, language was a problem, so we chiefly managed with hand gestures, pencils and paper. I hopped in and out of an Arab theatre, which had no roof, one not being necessary anyway. It had a very crude stage and hard seats but it was fun watching the artists, who appeared to be moaning in Arabic, yet the Arabs were laughing their heads off. Ah well, so be it. We had a do-it-yourself concert in the desert. The occasion was that a battalion of Tommies had arrived from Mesopotamia and they were crazy with happiness because they were on their way home after years of operations in the Arabian Desert.

We laid on plenty of beer, 'eats' and tobacco and made a rough and ready welcome. Our scratch band provided some music with banjos, mandolins, and even a piano was mysteriously rustled up. We had a good singsong and for a moment officers and men seemed on a level, all of which the Tommies enjoyed very much. After the party we sent them off to their troopship, marching to the tune 'Rolling home to Merrie England'. So away they went all smiles and in good cheer on their way to their loved ones at home.

When we arrived back on board in the early evening what a spectacle caught our eyes. It amazed us to see that a huge oil tanker was on fire. What a frightening sight with jet-black smoke rising in immense clouds. The flames were awful. There was feverish activity close at hand and all ships and crews were doing what they could to quench the fire. Burning oil surrounded the vessel and some of her crew were trapped in their quarters unable to get out of the portholes, which were not big enough. They were going mad, as the heat must have been torturous.

Hoses were passed through to keep the bulkheads from getting red hot. Then the authorities decided to tow her to open sea, as she was a danger to the closely moored ships. What a pity oxyacetylene cutters had not been invented, which would have enabled holes to be cut in the tankers hull, but no, it could not be.

Those terrified faces at the portholes will remain in my memory always. Some thought that the Marines should have been ordered to shoot them to save further agony, but in the end drugs were passed to them. Oh how helpless we all were. The tanker burnt herself out, completely down to the water's edge, a pitiful sight indeed and the unfortunate crew, of course, were burnt to death. It upset everyone, being so helpless.

We left our moorings and proceeded to Alexandria, which is about 100 miles west of Port Said and situated on the River Nile Delta. This is an ancient city full of historic interest, where excavations were always taking place. I was able to watch, with fascination, what was going on. In the town there was a large and beautiful museum full of interesting objects dating back to the Pharaohs' time. It struck me rather curious that although there were so many of these exhibits dated B.C. or early A.D. that the years from 1,000 A.D. seemed such a blank space. The sarcophaguses and statues were wonderful works of art. The carvings in white marble and alabaster were exquisite, certainly far better than modern sculpture. When one thinks of the crude methods the ancients had and their makeshift tools it is difficult to conceive how such masterpieces could emerge. Patience and craftsmanship stood out as an example to us all. When I see monstrosities that are called contemporary, or abstract art, and read the glib way of explaining the sculptor's work, to me I think it is trashy and that the artists are taking the public for a ride. To feast my eyes on the ancient sculpture was indeed wonderful, as I love to see personal endeavour which has been carried out by hand.

Strolling around Alexandria in temperatures of 100 degrees in the shade was very tiring, but any inconvenience caused by the heat was offset by the quaintness of the buildings and their shady interiors which kept the sun out. Poverty and disease seemed commonplace, because, I suppose, the natives knew no better. I thought we had awful slums at home, until I visited such places as Alexandria.

However, the bazaars were full of interest with everyone selling or making articles. By the River Nile there were women doing their washing, wearing just loincloths, and nothing else. Infants were straddling their mothers' shoulders and hanging onto their hair. Whilst mothers knelt down bashing clothes on the rocks to clean them, their babies would have to hang on like grim death. I actually saw one mother, whilst walking along, hand her breast to an infant to have its 'elevenses'. These poor wretches appeared to have no modesty at all. They even gave birth to their babies wherever the mother happened to be at the time. But they managed, although, no doubt, the death rate was high. Conditions were certainly primitive, "Where were the men folk?" you ask. Well, they would be playing curious games or smoking in groups from their hubble-bubbles. When the sun went down, and temperatures dropped, they would start selling their wares and engage in their crafts of mat making and weaving. Sunset was always a lovely sight with the warm red glow silhouetting the mosques and white buildings. It was all so tranquil, unless you were in a market or bazaar, with its weird music, nude dancers, and constant babble of Arabic tongues, and oh that smell. Will I ever forget it? Perhaps, sometimes there would be just a waft of perfume, for which I was very grateful.

On the outskirts of the town, in a lovely setting of date palms and exotic plants, was a zoo with fine specimens of lions and other animals.

We saw the prison, where prisoners sat in concrete cages facing the street behind iron bars. On the street sat relatives, waiting with sad faces, to supply the prisoners with food. The food was scanty and looked horrible.

Transport here was mainly by trams, pulled by mules, and camels. It was interesting to see a caravan coming from the desert – a formidable waste of sand – the horizon would be blurred by a heat haze and the wind would make the sand look like the swell on an ocean. Talking of wind, when a sand storm occurred it could be uncomfortable and even frightening. In our conventional attire the hot sand would get everywhere and stick to the sweat of one's body. The caravanners were always dressed from head to foot in loose clothes, with headgear designed so that they could cover up when a sand storm occurred. Their sandals turned up at the toes and skidded over the loose sand whilst, with our footwear, the hot sand penetrated everywhere, making our feet very uncomfortable. We did try walking backwards in order to avoid getting too much sand on our face and neck. Now to relate a further experience of a sandstorm and an event which would put me in the limelight aboard the *Ceres*.

    I was on watch in the boiler room one afternoon in a stifling temperature of 110 degrees; there was just one boiler alight for supplying steam to dynamos, refrigeration plants and for domestic uses, when a sandstorm arose in all its fury. We lay at anchor in the bay and it became so rough that we began dragging our anchor, which was a dangerous situation, if it could not be checked. I was the petty officer of the watch and I received instructions over the phone from the engineer commander in the engine room, "Petty officer Smith, this is an order, listen intently: raise steam for fifteen knots in thirty minutes." I knew that this normally took two or three hours. Then he added, "I take full responsibility for any damage you may incur. I want that steam. Can you manage?"

    "Give me two more stokers," I replied, "and I'll do my utmost." My rank was only *acting* petty officer, and I was very young, but my previous study of machinery stood me in good stead.

    I knew what I had to do. Hell was let loose. What with the roaring of oil burning at full output and the unnerving pulsation, shouting orders was ludicrous, so I used signs with hands and fingers to signal to the stokers. I knew the risks I was running, "Smudge," I said to myself, "this is your chance to show all and sundry what you can do, or at least give them confidence in you."

Minutes passed by. I was furnishing the cold boiler with its thirty tons of water, and how I watched those gauges for signs of power! Then, in just fifteen minutes, there was a flicker of power. In the engine room all eyes were watching my efforts on their gauges. The turbines were warming up but the ship was moving closer towards rocks. I had no time to worry and was wringing wet with sweat, but from the heat, not fear. I never thought about bursting the boiler but had to use all my 'know-how'. The lieutenant commander came down and shouted in my ear,

"Carry on, I trust you lad, I won't interfere!" and so I did. After only twenty minutes of this strain, I called the engine room, "I am connecting B2 boiler now." I said, "Stand by!" Then, I opened up the main stop valve, whilst wondering what might happen. The two boilers equalised and the telegraph changed to, 'slow ahead'. The pressure dropped, but with a bit of work, I soon recovered that. But the heat was becoming too intense, I wondered if I might I pass out. Then, after a few minutes, which seemed like hours, I had the signal, 'Stop'. That meant that I had to act quickly and shut off the oil supply. The safety valves lifted with a shattering noise but gently I regained control of the pressure. The telegraph rang, 'Finished with main engines'. I was feeling whacked but I had succeeded.

All the steelwork was too hot to touch with temperatures of 140 degrees. Oh, for a breath of air. A relief was soon sent down to the boiler room to take over from me and I went on deck. I was as red as a beetroot, as were my three stokers. I was met by the commander, who took me aft to the Ward Room where he shook my hand and said, "Well done, lad, now drink this Whisky and Lemon." And me a teetotaller! But at least it was a drink. I was ordered to rest and see the captain in the morning.

Next morning, when I explained to the engineering officers what I had done, I was congratulated and told that I was now to see the captain. The commander explained what had happened, and the captain straight away confirmed me in my rank as petty officer. The captain said that rapid promotion would be sure to follow and that, when the *Ceres* commission was over, I would be sent to the engineering College to train as an engineer lieutenant. But would that be the case? I will explain later.

I had been keeping my 'mail for home' up to date but somehow our 'mail from home' was chasing us from country to country. It was November and as I lay in my hammock, my thoughts, were thousands of miles away. In view of the expected happy event I was wondering what was happening and wished that I could be with Louisa, handy and on the spot. However that could not be.

Chapter 25 – Russia and news from home.

We received an urgent signal to proceed to Mersina in Turkish Asia Minor due north of the Levant, which skirted Palestine. Off we went at 25-30 knots. Apparently it had been reported that the Armenian Turks were massacring Christians. It was an SOS and there were about 500 miles to go. We arrived the next day and landed fully armed Marines and bluejackets who marched through the small town of Mersina. They discovered that it was seemingly a false alarm, and everything appeared peaceful.

How strange it is that in certain places different religions clash in bloodshed and holy wars. Would people be more prepared to co-exist, and be more amiable, without religion, a subject on which there is so much study and preaching? It is just my opinion, but I believe these people commit the gravest sin of self-satisfaction in their own creeds and make holiness and brotherhood of man a farce. As I have said before I am confused and mixed up when I weigh up different religions. Out there, around parts of the Mediterranean, it seems so easy to start trouble. Even in Palestine, the custodian of the Holy Sepulcher, Arabs and Jews are always in conflict. But there, I must not criticize too much.

After a few days, with no leave ashore, we returned to Alexandria and prepared for another trip, this time to Constantinople, with a stop at Famagusta, in Cyprus. We went ashore to get provisions, to refuel and, incidentally, to get some Christmas fare, because we would be going to places that had no such things. After that we proceeded to Cyprus at about 18 knots. We found that Cyprus had a spicy smell and there were quite a variety of things grown there. It was a lovely island, with a mixture of Greek and Turkish people. Again there were two religions casting their deadly spell over their followers and causing distrust and enmity. We left after a brief stay and, back at sea, noticed that temperatures were dropping as winter loomed. How busy the *Ceres* was. She was my young lady, she made me feel very proud and I loved her. Ah well, after leaving Famagusta we hugged the coast steaming westward past the Isle of Rhodes. We then veered north, through the Grecian Archipelago, with its ruggedness and beauty. Approaching the Dardanelles the weather began to deteriorate. In fact, it became very cold and made me think of old England.

Veering eastwards through the Dardanelles we saw snow on the mountains, which was a chilly thought after months of beautiful warm sunshine, and persuaded us to get our woollies out again. Once more we went through the Sea of Marmara to an island and anchored at a town called Prinkipo. This was where Turkish Aristocrats went gambling in casinos. It was a very pretty place with white buildings amidst the green trees growing on the hillsides. At night the lights ashore gave a twinkling effect as the trees moved their branches. Ashore it seemed clean, but to avoid clashes with the Turks, we were not allowed any leave.

We were awaiting orders and becoming impatient about our lack of mail. I, especially, was wondering how Louisa was faring, was I, or was I not, a father yet? I suppose one always fears the worst. I asked my Jimmy the One, my first lieutenant, if I would get any news or cable. "Why?" he asked. When I told him, his said, "I'm in the same boat as you are. So, let me know when you have any news and we'll both celebrate." He later became an Admiral of the Fleet, Sir Arthur John Power, a grand fellow.

We moved on to Constantinople and anchored near the Sultan's Palace. What a change we saw, snow had been followed by a thaw and the streets were in a ghastly mess. I went ashore in sea boots, wading inches deep in slushy muck. I will refrain from describing in detail how deplorable it was but still I had to be nosy and see for myself. We found a clean looking café, I think that it was in the English colony of Pera, and we spent some time in there before returning aboard.

After refuelling, replenishing stores, sending some mail home, and still not receiving any, we up-anchored and steamed east into the Black Sea along with two destroyers as companions. The weather was getting very cold indeed and by the time we arrived at Sebastopol, in the Crimea, there were signs of ice on deck.

However, it seemed we were not to settle there, and although we were not informed of our mission, we knew it was something important. I heard afterwards that as we patrolled the west coast waiting for orders, the battleship *Ajax* and our sister ship *Caradoc* together with several other destroyers were east of the Crimea in the Sea of Azov. We did manage to go ashore a few times and, through an interpreter, were able to converse with the Cossacks. They were friendly and there seemed to be no suspicion of us. Since we were not at war with Russia we carried no arms. But Russia was in a terrible state of revolution. It was a time when control and government were useless and orders were issued day by day, by commissars, some of whom, it seemed, had forgotten the quality of mercy. The Russian people did not really trust anyone. They dared not speak, were dejected, afraid to smile and were nearly starving, and all this with the Russian winter descending with a vengeance. To make things worse there was scarcely any fuel, and very often the lighting would fail, water supplies were interrupted, shops were bare and many people were wearing rags.

As Christmas neared, I was getting a little worried by not hearing any news. We returned to Constantinople and a strange sight met our eyes; ships were lying at anchor in the Golden Horn but were spread-eagled, with some pointing east and some west. We learned that the Russian rivers had frozen over, so that the ten-knot current had ceased and the sea was still. This was the first time in seventeen years that it had happened.

We anchored, took some special agents aboard and, best of all and at last, our mail had caught up with us, and there was plenty of it. Yes, there was the letter I had waited for telling me that I had a daughter. Rosina Alice Louisa, born on November 12th. I think I was struck a little silly, because I rushed aft to see Jimmy the One. "Mine's a girl!" I blurted out. He was all smiles, took my hand and shaking it said, "Congratulations, so is mine. Let's make a toast." After a chat, and a couple of whiskies and sodas, I went forward, told my messmates and, after all sorts of ribbing, said,

"I'll break my temperance rule. There is some rum in my locker; let's wet the baby's head." I certainly wetted my head, and felt drunk pretty quickly, no matter, it was a rare occasion, and I was excited. There were a few others with similar news, so we had quite a "to-do". It appears that a cable for me had gone astray on its way to Alexandria. I now had a bundle of letters galore with numerous dates. Some were scolding me for not answering, although I had written, whenever it had been possible to get a letter posted. Louisa was rather sad and upset at my absence. It made me wonder if perhaps sailors should not marry, lest their ship, in my case the *Ceres,* should steal their affections. I must confess I loved my ship, and why not, she was my home and a staunch friend. Silly talk but it was how my emotions were going. How Louisa implored me in her letters to get home, even if I had to buy myself out of the Royal Navy, I knew that I must write to her and re-assure her. Now you will read how it all happened.

At that time, whilst in harbour, an Admiralty order was posted on the notice board to the effect that, despite demobilization, the Navy had too many petty officers and chiefs. Anyone who wished could have a free discharge and go onto the reserve list. My messmate, Bob Gillis, who was also married, said, "Smudge, if you are game, so am I." So we both applied for free-discharges. At my interview, the engineer commander did his best to discourage me in view of their intentions to promote me to officer grade. I listened to him and hesitated. After all, the Navy had made me, it was my career, until, that is, romance came into my life, and now I was thinking of home. I was hoping for some guidance, hoping that telepathy would play a part, and that I would find some intuitive response. I pondered and weighed the pros and cons. Could I ever be a commissioned officer with no bank balance and with my background? What was it to be, ambition or love? I kept thinking of that baby that I had not yet seen, and of my Louisa who I loved.

I told the officers, that I did appreciate their help and that I was sorry if I had let them down. However grim life might be at home, I felt that was where my duty lie. However, I thought that if the Navy felt that they needed me, they would never grant me a free discharge. "But," I thought, "I must try to get home." and I put my name on the list to await an Admiralty decision.

   The next day was Christmas Day 1919. We had what celebrations we could, but, owing to the snow, there was no dancing on the upper deck. However, the band, which was getting quite good by then, played below decks in the warm. We had cinema shows too, coupled with our own on-board comedians, whose comments would not be passed by any censor. The lads all had a good time and let their hair down. The food was far better than our previous Christmas when we had been in north Russia. Then it was biscuits and bully-beef, this year we had turkey. Our cooks did us proud cooking our turkey in Turkey.

   It was a very happy Christmas Day and I felt on top of the world. Until, that is, I thought of someone far away pining for me. I had been torn between love and duty. Was I right to try and leave the Navy? Perhaps, somehow I had grown to hate the sea, which I had chosen to make my career, a career in which I had made good progress. I thought that eventually something will happen, and my course will or will not be altered.

   Meanwhile, we had taken on board extra clothing, blankets, arms and plenty of stoves and I wondered, "What's going on now?" The weather was getting colder when we weighed anchor and steamed northeast, and the sea became covered in ice floes. The next day we arrived off the Russian city and port of Odessa.

   For fifteen miles we pushed through the sea ice, frozen into petrified wavelets. It was a fascinating sight, especially when the sun peeped through, and the ice glistened. Although, looking a nice sight, it left me with an unpleasant feeling. As the ice got thicker it piled up on our bows, even coming onto our forecastle, and eventually it brought us to a halt. Our orders had been to go into the harbour, so a Russian icebreaker was requested to assist us in getting in. However, the icebreaker's crew refused to help us. Some of our bluejackets jumped onto the ice, ran to the icebreaker and compelled her by force of arms to accede to our request, which eventually they did, albeit sulkily.

Meanwhile we were charging at the ice, backwards and forwards, thrusting our bows into it and causing long cracks. The noise of the crushing ice was terrific but as it passed alongside it froze at our stern and we could not move any further. The commandeered icebreaker now went into action and my word she did her stuff alright. We were able to follow her inside and eventually moored alongside a mole, or quay, which was crowded with Russians. Some of our Tommies ashore gave us a rousing cheer for they felt safe with our white ensign arriving. Strict sentry duty was imposed, which was a bitterly cold duty, it being 30 degrees below zero. It proved especially difficult for us, because only a week ago we were basking in the 90s. Now it was a case of wearing two of everything. What a horrible contrast. And oh, how it showed what our bodies could really take. To add to this desolate scene, it snowed hard, three or four feet of the stuff, which then froze. One thing, however, it was dry.

How women and children stood up to this, I will never know. They were also victims of the Revolution which was to rend a huge country apart. All because of man's inhumanity to man. Will the people of this Earth ever understand each other's problems? I hope to God our dear old England will never see a revolution like that. Why, oh why, do aristocrats have to drive poor people to such straits? One has only to see the misery and degradation that is caused by selfishness and greed. When will human beings ever learn? But I am afraid, perhaps, they never will.

Well, it seems our sympathies, were with the White Russians. When I say, "our sympathies", I mean "our Government's sympathies". We were alongside the pier in the docks and it was time to take stock. Near us lie destroyers of other nations awaiting to take off their refugees, but everyone was held fast by the ice. It was so cold that water froze immediately, and everywhere was thick snow and ice. On the quay were a few hundred Russians in pitiful clothing, clutching personal belongings in bundles and looking forlorn and without hope. These poor devils were the victims of the civil war, which had followed the Russian Revolution, and had almost given up hope, until seeing us arrive. They thought that we had come to help them in their plight.

Odessa was a big city but it now looked bare and desolate, which was such a pity. Double sentries, armed with machine guns, were posted on the jetties, with just two-hour duties, owing to extreme cold. Some military officers came aboard, who were part of a British mission which we were to help in any way we could. A few Tommies also embarked and told us some hair-raising stories. So we knew what to expect ashore. The captain told us that we could have an afternoon leave ashore but must return by early evening, and that there would be no all-night leave. Then we had a pep talk from the fleet surgeon telling us of the various diseases prevalent ashore, such as typhus, dysentery, cholera and, he stressed, venereal disease. The talk was enough to scare anyone, warning us always to have in mind our wives and sweethearts at home. Yes, it was sound advice.

We were not to be armed and were urged, as we might be mixing with rebels and loyalists, to be as impartial as possible, and always to be on our guard. As that first evening drew on there came an east wind with heavy snow, which was torture to be out in, and not too far away we could hear machine gun and rifle fire. Below decks, however, we were snug and warm.

The next day I went ashore with a party of men to have a look around the city of Odessa. There seemed to be Russian soldiers on guard on every street. They were Cossacks, I think, and they looked dejected and haggard. To help with the language difficulty, I had a small book of translated Russian phrases that proved useful. From the docks we went up an incline and came to a Square, where stood some public buildings, including an opera house, which, we were told, was now used as a torture chamber by whichever side, White or Red, were the masters at the time.

It was all quiet as we looked at the lovely buildings but we were feeling the cold. Then we met a couple of Tommies with a Jewish interpreter, a man who was very helpful. We followed the Tommies down what had been a main street and into a big hotel. A once lavish place, with a sort of Palm Court orchestra. Once inside the Tommies ordered drinks and, just to see how far it would go, we exchanged one English pound, and got 2,000 roubles for it. Well, it seemed we were millionaires. There were only a few customers in the hotel and all around us was broken furniture, and evidence of shooting. There was a fireplace, without a fire, and it was terribly cold. They appeared to be without heating everywhere. Looking out into the street, deep with snow, we saw an occasional troika glide by, which were like taxicabs on skids. These, and various other types of sleighs, were all drawn by horses. It was indeed a strange sight. To turn a corner in one of these vehicles was a work of art, because, of course, a sledge has no steering mechanism, apart from the horses, and it was, therefore, a case of slithering round erratically.

To get our feet warm, a few of us went out for a walk round the town. There were not many food shops, and other shops were bare of goods for sale. What little they did have, by Russian standards, was very expensive. For instance, a loaf of bread was ten roubles. To me, at that time, that was the equivalent of three-ha'pence but pre-war a rouble had been valued at around three shillings. However, there would be worse experiences of inflation in store for us. We pooled our cash each day and, if we did buy anything, one chap would do it all. We tried to use all our cash and never hold any over until the next day.

Some shops were filled with photographs of people who had been tortured by the Reds. With pictures of young men with their thumbs twisted round to stop them gripping a rifle, others had feet hacked off and many others told a horrific tale of torture. It was really awful. As evening drew on, the wind freshened and snow started falling again, so we rejoined the main party, went back on board, and were glad to get some warmth.

The White Russians, having heard that the British navy had arrived, were infiltrating into the city. Maybe they too, had a gleam of hope of rescue. There also were the Red Russians who were sending secret agents into the town. Mostly they always came in the night, when there would be sniping and murder going on. At that time we were not aware of our purpose in the town, indeed, it was being kept a secret. All we knew was that we were to rescue the Tommies if the Reds over-run the city.

The White Russian men were nervy and scared, and had lost all heart for fighting. So our Marines taught the young teenagers, both boys and girls, how to use weapons to defend their city. They were given a promise that they would be taken off by our ships, at the last extreme. Women and girls had their hair cut short and were dressed as men. A real awkward squad they were too, but they were a determined lot.

The electric power would be cut off without any warning, mostly caused by a scarcity of fuel, and this caused more apprehension and fear. Clean snow was used for drinking water, as it was hygienically safer to use any other. After a couple of days our bluejackets had become an attraction and there seemed to be even more people in the city.

One afternoon in the hotel we were having a coffee, served with Benedictine for a good warming effect, when our table was visited by a tall Cossack officer, whose uniform had seen better days. Through our interpreter we were asked to accompany him to a secluded room, which we did. Inside there were two more Cossacks on guard and we were beckoned to sit down facing two high-ranking officers in full uniforms, which were also rather shabby. They told us that they were General Denikin and General Wrangel and that they wanted to chat with us. Firstly, we asked, via the interpreter, if they could order some food and drink, but were told that we would have to entertain them, because they were without any cash. So we stood the treat. They said they hoped we would give the Loyalists a better heart to fight and regretted they could not entertain us, as they were living from day to day hoping we could help them. All the Russians were armed with knives, pistols and rifles, were all over six feet tall and all looked very menacing. But we could see they were dejected and had lost the heart to fight. We noticed that the least noise they heard caused them to get agitated, their nerves were on edge. The 'generals' explained that though we were not at war with the Reds, our presence was a boost to the White Russians' morale. They warned us about counterfeit notes which we had already learned about, to our sorrow. We were also told that should we be offered any note over fifty Roubles, sixpence to us, we should get the signature of the giver, which would be quite a performance. The British Consul had been very helpful, changing dud notes for us. We left the room with cordial handshakes and resumed our place in the restaurant.

We then noticed some pitifully clad teenage girls, sitting at empty tables, who looked very sad and miserable. Their top boots were nearly worn out and they wore tatty furs to keep some warmth in their bodies. Through our interpreter we invited the girls to our tables and asked them if they were hungry, which they were. So a meal was arranged. Then we asked them why, being such young girls, they were in this hotel. What we learned was awful. One girl was the daughter of a surgeon and his wife and they lived in two rooms of a large mansion, while all the other rooms were empty. It seems pieces of furniture had been taken to the commissariat, a sort of pawnbroker, which was trying to sell the wares but the city was so desperate that there was no money for furniture. While the sale of the goods lagged, the owners were getting hungrier. They had lowered the price that they had been asking for, but all to no avail. It transpired that these girls were so desperate to get money for their family they would be willing to sell their bodies to the British, as we were, by their standards, rich. We heard similar harrowing stories from others which filled us with pity. I was thinking thank goodness our girls at home are not in the same plight, how awful that would be to envisage.

It seems one seaman, from another table, slipped out and went to a nearby hotel, following a girl who had left for a rendezvous a little earlier. However after twenty minutes, or so, he returned very upset and ashamed. He said as he approached her on the bed she had drawn a revolver and shot herself rather than face the shame. Well, as I have said before, we always spent the money which we had changed the same day. So, along with some mates, I went round the tables and collected everyone's small change. We raised 1,000 roubles, only ten shillings to us, and this was shared out between the girls. They were very grateful for the money and that we had not taken advantage of them.

I was trying to think of something else that we could do to help, but what on earth was there? I remembered our fleet surgeon's remarks, "Always have your wives and sweethearts in mind." If there be a merciful God may he spare our dear country these horrors for they would seem too terrible to endure. Gazing upon this once beautiful city, suffering so much and now all in the throes of a bitter winter, "What a boon peace and tranquillity can be." I thought. But fortunately tempers change, wars end and there follows a slow climb back to sanity.

Our folks at home were suffering in a different way, with many thousands of unemployed. Those who were not called up were still in their cushy jobs, whilst the one-time heroes, Tommy and Jack, were now demobilised and demoralised, and, apart from those near and dear to them, what did anyone care? Maybe the rich were even sorry the war was now over. Such is civilization, I suppose.

I was beginning to wonder if I should I have applied for my discharge from the Navy. But maybe I was just fed up with this Arctic weather.

Back in the Hotel, it was late afternoon and we were preparing to leave. There was a heavy snowstorm in progress, whipped up by an easterly gale, and the heavy clouds made it look very dark. As usual, the evening orchestra of machine gun and rifle fire struck up. Snow, piled up in the streets, was so white that it exposed us in our dark blue uniforms to any snipers. We paused, and then discovered that the entrance to the hotel was under fire.

A Russian tried to leave the hotel but fell, hit by a sniper's bullet. We had to get out somehow. Then the lights went out, cut off at the power station. Firing broke out inside our hotel. It was so near that we had to crouch down near a plate glass window. We decided to make our way in twos and threes, and at intervals. We smashed the plate glass window and waited for a lull in the firing. It came to my turn and I went out with Bob. We hugged the walls of the buildings and made for the square. There was occasional firing and the driver of a sledge coming down the road was shot, and probably killed, by a sniper. Had it been one of our boys, I suppose, we would have risked our lives but we decided it was no business of ours. As Bob and I stood against the wall of the Opera House we heard screams and moans from some poor devils who were being tortured inside, which, of course was making us even more nervous. But the *Ceres* was only a half a mile away!

We decided to cross the open square and Bob went first, while I waited. There was a plop of a bullet against the wall, which I was standing by, followed by the report from a rifle. My heart beat quicker. What should I do next? I looked across the square at the wilderness of snow, and again there was the thud of a bullet followed by a flash and report from a rifle. I could see a dim figure by a lamppost and could hear a guttural laugh. I shouted,

"Prooski oldat... Engliske matrors." There was no reply. I waited until there were no more shots and then walked towards the gunman, with my hands raised. My only thought was to convince, whoever it was, not to shoot me! As I neared him, I shouted again,

"Engliske matrors!"

"Kharasko!" he said, which meant "good" – I hoped! I walked up to him and saw that he was a tall Cossack, with a rifle and an automatic pistol. And me unarmed! However, "so far so good." I thought. He looked me over and then seemed to relax. I tried to stay composed, and to keep talking. I offered him a cigarette,

"Innye Engliske Papieros," I said, offering him a cigarette.

"Dah!" he said, taking one,

"Mraye Speeoki," he asked. I gave him a box of matches and while he fumbled with cold fingers, I offered to hold his rifle. I noticed it was an English rifle made by Ross.

"Ross Engliske," I said, opening the bolt and removing the bullet,

"Can I keep the bullet for a souvenir?" I asked.

"Dah" he said. Then he drew his automatic pistol, saying, "Deutsch" and passed it to me to have a look. It was a Steyr automatic and loaded.

"Now," I thought, "what should I do? Kill him?" I decided, however, to retreat and slowly, holding his rifle in one hand and his automatic in the other, I backed away from him. He did not move. Then, when I was some distance from him, I called out, threw his rifle into the snow and continued walking away from him, backwards. He did not venture to follow. So, that was that. Phew! And now for home.

Bob was far ahead by now. So I ran and slid like a child on a toboggan down the hill to our ship. And did I slide well, on knees and on my bottom. Suddenly I noticed that I was warm. It must have been all the excitement. I arrived, out of breath, at the base of the hill, where Russians were spilling out of a café, all too busy arguing to see me. Now I could see the docks, with their railway trucks, only fifty yards away. I suddenly stopped, my path blocked by a pack of wild dogs, looking more like wolves, with their tongues hanging out. Now what, I thought? Then it came to me: all the firing in the town meant that our sentries would have been posted by the jetty. I called out and one of our sentries answered asking me who I was. I told him and explained about the dogs. The sentry opened up with his Lewis gun, scared the pariah dogs away and shouted, "Come on, Smudge!" Was I relieved?

Bob and all the others also had to use their cunning and wits to scrape aboard. I kept the Steyr automatic, the gun which might have ended my life, if providence had not been on my side. A few words of Russian on that occasion had been a godsend. What an afternoon that was, and one to be remembered.

After a hot meal the ship's company was alerted that something was afoot. There was heavy firing coming from shore and we could see fires burning. The townspeople, with their few personal belongings, were flocking down towards the docks and our ship, threatening to overwhelm us. But they were checked when we trained our machine guns and our six-inch guns towards them. There were some other foreign destroyers, also frozen in, and which were taking their own nationals aboard, but we made it clear, via an interpreter, that only the wounded would be allowed aboard our ship. Some Russians resorted to self-mutilation by shooting their own feet and hands. In the sick bay we found out that some of the injured were women with their hair cut short and in soldier's uniform. In fact, we discovered, quite a lot were women and girls, who were crying and screaming for their husbands. Our main problem was that our Tommies were still fighting their way out through the docks. It seemed a mass exodus from Odessa was taking place, with the wealthy even bringing their new motor cars – Rolls and Bentleys – all being pushed onto the ice. Some of our Tommies were guided to a spot, just outside town, where our destroyers could pick them up, while others came to us. What a filthy state our lads were in, and how grateful they were to enjoy a hot bath and clean underwear, while we washed all their clothes.

It seemed that the British at first had hoped to assist in a rescue of the Tsar and his family but they had been murdered. Now the British were giving support to the last of the White Russian forces. But our Tommies suffering had been all in vain. When night fell it was pitiful, with temperatures of more than 30 degrees below. Those poor devils out there and most of them not at all suitably dressed. It made us all very agitated; we could not take any more on board because we were already crowded out. The bitter cold wind claimed many victims, who had to be left where they fell and our cordons of sentries were kept very busy forcing the crowd back. In desperation, our ship opened fire, over the Russians' heads, yet still they surged towards us. Looking across the city during the night we could see bright flashes of field guns lighting up the sky. The Red Army were on the outskirts of Odessa, and in force. The battleship *Ajax*, laying off shore, was given the range of the Reds and sent a salvo of fifteen-inch shells, which burst on the distant hills. In the cold still air, the shattering roar of those guns was deafening and the hills echoed with this "hell let loose". Unfortunately, the bombardment did not stop the Red Army which then advanced into Odessa in force. News of this now started a real panic on shore, where mass hysteria was only too evident, as the poor devils hoped against hope for rescue.

Our captain was in a real dilemma, wanting to help the suffering people, but knowing full well we could not take any more. Then some women got onto the ice pleading to us for help. Oh how awful it was to feel so powerless, and I know our captain was overcome with emotion. I thought what an awful decision he would have to make. He ordered that if any attempt was made to rush the ship he would not hesitate to fire. Our guns were trained on the jetty where maybe a thousand people were collapsing and perishing with the cold and where others were even committing suicide. The crowd were so terribly frightened perhaps to them death did not matter anymore.

The icebreaker had been commandeered again and, together with all the other ships, which would follow in her wake, she was raising steam. This was a relief, at least for us, to know that preparations were being made to evacuate Odessa and leave the horror ashore to the will of the Red Army. God knows what was in store for those poor devils, being left without hope, warmth or comfort. Our kindest thoughts could not help them, and we could only offer succour to the wounded. But during the night, the soldiers, boys and girls really, who had been trained by us in the hope that they might save the city from the Red Army, and who we had promised rescue, should things go wrong, entered the docks by coming along the coast. A struggle ensued as we began to try and honour our promise and embark them on board. Fighting broke out on the jetty and we had to pull up the gangways and again threaten to fire. Then in haste, and feverish activity, we put explosive charges under the ice, and with that, and the work of the icebreaker battering at the ice, we managed to slowly steam out of the port. The date was February 7th 1920.

Never will I forget that scene in Odessa. There was us, with all the good will that we could muster, and there were those poor people hoping for a miracle. But the days of miracles, it seemed, had long ago passed.

If the Almighty can really hear prayers, then he must have heard many that day, but why, oh why, was there no sign? I have battled many times with my conscience as to whether God cares for his children as much as the clergy would have us believe. I suppose I can understand why my small voice of prayer remained unheard that day, but the noise of those explosions, the gunfire and, worst of all, those hysterical screams from the dockside, how could that not be heard? Perhaps God was not there because we were really in Hell.

It is now fifty years later, and I have yet to find an answer. If there is one, let it be one of understanding and, above all, peace among innocent people.

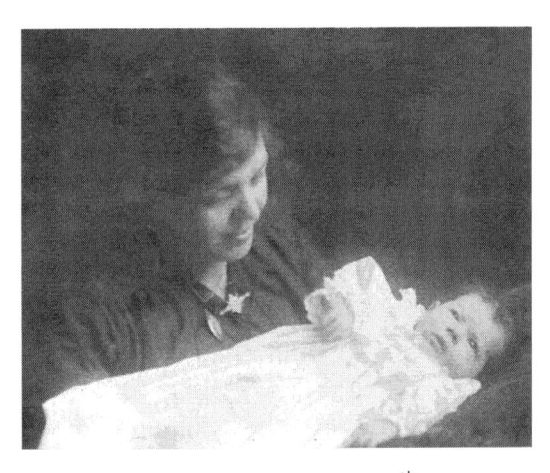

Louisa with baby Rosina – born 12th November 1919

Postscript

Fred finished his story as his ship steamed out of Odessa on February 7th 1920. Perhaps he intended writing more, but none has been discovered.

In 1920, 'Smudge' returned to live in Camberwell, London with his wife Louisa and baby daughter Rosina, having accepted his free discharge from the Royal Navy. He and Louisa received a present of a christening dress for Rosina from the rescued Mrs Hill, who had returned to Riga after the war.

He remained a Royal Naval Reservist for ten years, which involved him in regular refresher courses at Chatham. He worked for the General Post Office, and became an engineer with the developing telephone and communication systems. After his final naval discharge, he was able to use his £500 Royal Navy pay-off to buy a new semi-detached suburban house, with a large garden in a quiet cul-de-sac in Sidcup, Kent. He continued to commute to London until his retirement.

Fred's only child Rosina joined the London Fire Service during the Second World War, and in 1946, she married Adrian Robinson. When she cleared his house in 1970, after Fred's death, Rosina found 'Smudge's Story', written in school exercise books. After many years Rosina's only child, Wendy helped by her sister-in-law, typed up the handwritten account.

As Fred tells us he and his brother George had married two sisters, Louisa and Alice Bence. George and Alice lived in Plaistow, East London, after the War, where George died in the 1950s and Alice in the '60s. They had two sons, George Junior, who died serving in the army in 1943, a Prisoner of War on the Burma-Siam railway, and Jack, who married Lil and had six children.

Fred's oldest sister Ella had six children. Her youngest daughter, born in 1916, was called Jessamine, named after the sloop *HMS Jessamine* which Fred was serving on at the time. Fred's other sister Beatrice married Philip Simister and had a son also called Philip. They lived in Chelsea.

After Fred's beloved wife Louisa died in 1960, Fred continued to live in Sidcup enjoying his house and garden, and writing this story. He died peacefully in his sleep on 5th May 1970 aged 76.

Rosina, a few months before she died in 2002, and at the age of 83, presented a copy of 'Smudge's Story', along with pictures, Fred's pencil drawings and maps to the Imperial War Museum.

Now, in 2014, 'Smudge's Story' has been edited and published by his grand-daughter and great-nephew. It is hoped that this will allow Fred to tell his story to present members of his family and that it will remain available as a reminder to all of Fred's life and service, and of the lives and service of all those other millions who suffered in the Great War and its aftermath.

Fred's granddaughter, Wendy and Rosina present "Smudges Story" to Roderick Suddaby, Keeper of Documents at the Imperial War Museum.
February 2002.

Left to Right Jack Smith, Louisa, Fred (standing), Uncle Matt Haswell, Rosina, Matt's wife Frances, George, Alice, George Junior. Taken around 1923.

Rosina, Fred and Louisa on holiday in Ramsgate.

Fred and Louisa

Appendix i Family Tree

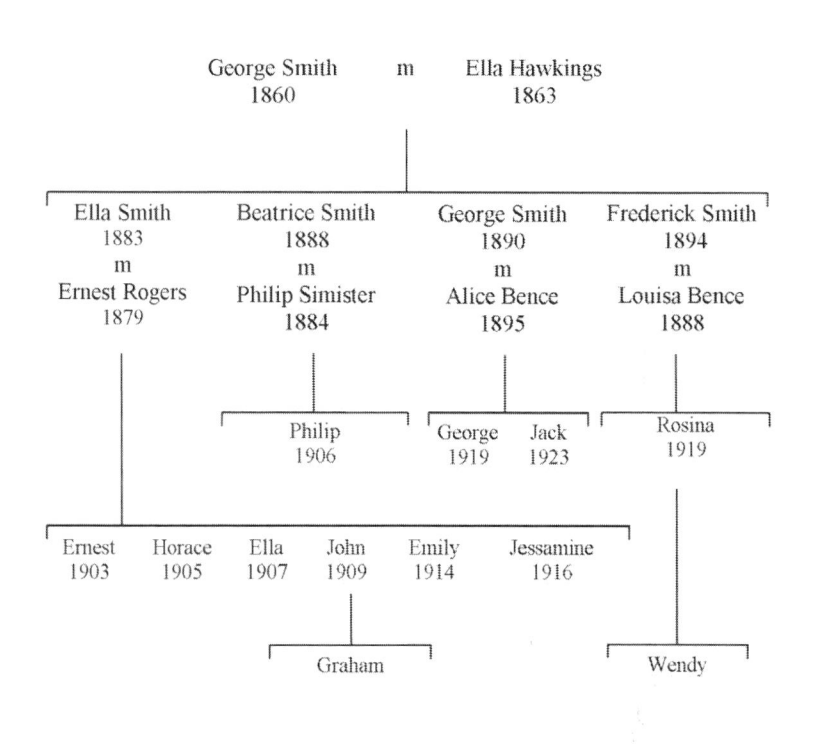

```
                    George Smith    m    Ella Hawkings
                         1860                 1863
                                  │
   ┌─────────────────┬────────────┴────────┬─────────────────┐
  Ella Smith      Beatrice Smith      George Smith      Frederick Smith
    1883              1888                1890               1894
      m                 m                   m                  m
 Ernest Rogers    Philip Simister       Alice Bence       Louisa Bence
    1879              1884                1895               1888
      │                 │                   │                  │
      │               Philip           ┌─────┴────┐          Rosina
      │               1906           George     Jack          1919
      │                                1919     1923
  ┌───┬───┬───┬───┬───┐                                        │
 Ernest Horace Ella John Emily Jessamine                    Wendy
  1903  1905  1907 1909 1914   1916
                     │
                  Graham
```

233

Appendix ii Fred's Naval Record

Appendix iii Alfred Bence

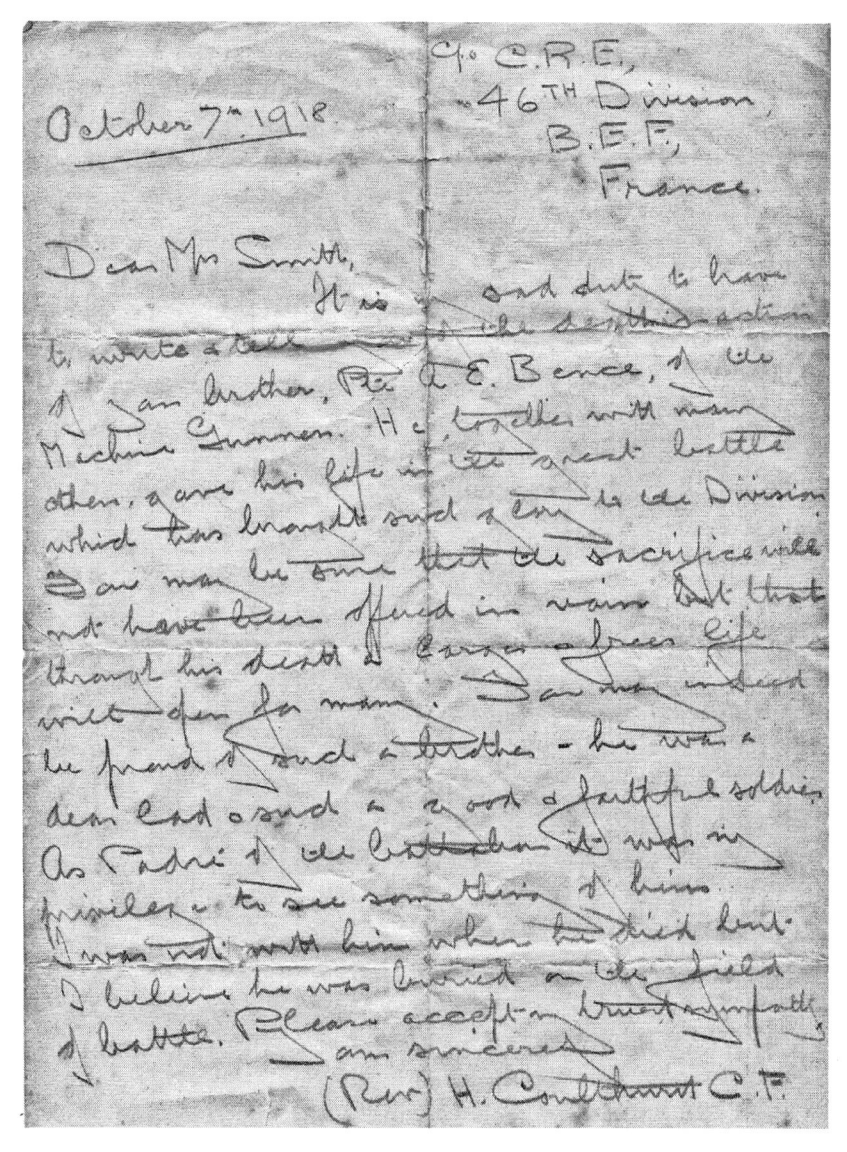

> C/o C.R.E.,
> 46th Division,
> B.E.F.,
> France.
>
> October 7th 1918
>
> Dear Mrs Smith,
>
> It is my sad duty to have to write a letter confirming the death in action of your brother, Pte A. E. Bence, of the Machine Gunners. He, together with many others, gave his life in the great battle which has brought such glory to the Division. One may be sure that the sacrifice will not have been offered in vain but that through his death a larger, freer life will open for many. You may indeed be proud of such a brother – he was a dear lad and such a good & faithful soldier. As Padre of the battalion it was my privilege to see something of him. I was not with him when he died but I believe he was buried on the field of battle. Please accept my truest sympathy.
>
> I am sincerely
> (Rev) H. Coulthurst C.F.

Letter to Louisa confirming her brother –
Alfred Bence – killed in France

October 7th 1918

c/o C.R.E.,
46th Division
B.F.E.,
France.

Dear Mrs Smith,

It is my sad duty to have to write and tell you of the death in action if your brother Pte A E **Bence of** the Machine Gunners. He, together with many others, gave his life in the great battle which has brought such glory to the Division. You may be sure that the sacrifice will not have been offered in vain but that through his death a larger freer life will open for many. You may indeed be proud if such a brother –he was a dear lad and such a good and faithful soldier. As padre of the Battalion it was my privilege to see something if him. I was not with him when he died but I believe he was buried on the field of battle. Please accept my truest sympathy.

I am sincerely

(Rev) H. Coulthurst C.F.

Official Army record:
Name: Alfred Ernest Bence
Birth Place: Battersea, Middx.
Death Date: 3 Oct 1918
Death Location: France & Flanders
Enlistment Location: Camberwell
Rank: Private
Regiment: Machine Gun Corps
Battalion: (Infantry)
Number: 45427
Type of Casualty: Killed in action
Theatre of War: Western European Theatre
Comments: Formerly R/18444, K.R.R.C

Men of the 46th Division on the banks of the St Quentin Canal
Could Alf be one of these machine gunners?

Printed in Great Britain
by Amazon.co.uk, Ltd.,
Marston Gate.